The Religion of Islam

Presented by the Qur'an and Sunnah

Prepared by:

Fahd ibn Hamad Al-Mubarak

Contents

In the Name of Allah, the Most Compassionate, the Most Merciful 3

Introduction 3

Dear reader: 7

1. The word of monotheism (there is no true god but Allah) 8

    b. Why did Allah create us? 14

2. Muhammad is the Messenger of Allah: 16

    a. What is the meaning of "messenger"? Who is Muhammad? And were there any messengers other than him? 16

    b. The first Messenger was our father Adam (peace be upon him): 17

    c. Noah (peace be upon him): 18

    d. Hūd (peace be upon him): 20

    e. Sālih (peace be upon him): 21

    f. Ibrāhim (Abraham) (peace be upon him): 22

    g. Lūt (Lot) (peace be upon him): 23

    h. Shu'ayb (peace be upon him): 23

    i. Mūsa (Moses) (peace be upon him): 24

    j. 'Isa (Jesus) (peace be upon him): 29

3. Muhammad, the Messenger of Allah (the seal of prophets and messengers) 33

    a. His lineage and honor 33

    b. His traits 33

    c. Quraysh and the Arabs 34

    d. The start of the Prophet's mission 34

    e. Supporting the Prophet with miracles: 43

    f. The noble Companions 44

4. The pillars of Islam 46

- a. First Pillar: The testimony that there is no god worthy of worship, but Allah and that Muhammad is the Messenger of Allah..................46
- b. Second Pillar: Establishing prayer 46
- c. Third Pillar: Zakah 47
- d. Fourth Pillar: Fasting the month of Ramadān 48
- e. Fifth Pillar: Performing Hajj 49
5. The Pillars of Faith...50
6. The teachings and morality of Islam..55
   - a. The Commands...55
     - First: Truthfulness of speech: 55
     - Second: Fulfillment of trusts, promises, and covenants, and acting justly among people:..56
     - Third: Being humble and refraining from arrogance:..........56
     - Fourth: Generosity and spending in charitable causes: 56
     - Fifth: Patience and enduring harm: 57
     - Sixth: Modesty: 57
     - Seventh: Dutifulness to one's parents: 58
     - Eighth: Treating people with good morals: 59
     - Ninth: Jihad in the cause of Allah to support the oppressed, establish the truth, and spread justice: 60
     - Tenth: Supplication, Dhikr, and Qur'an recitation:............60
     - Eleventh: Seeking religious knowledge, teaching it to others, and calling them to it:..62
     - Twelfth: Contentment with the judgment of Allah and His Messenger: 62
   - b. The Unlawful and Prohibited Things 63
     - First: Polytheism: Devoting any form of servitude to other than Allah Almighty: 63
     - Second: Magic, divination, and claiming to know the unseen:............64
     - Third: Injustice: 64

Fourth: Killing the soul made inviolable by Allah without right: 65
Fifth: Encroaching upon people's properties: 65
Sixth: Cheating, treachery, and betrayal: 66
Seventh: Attacking people's honor 66
Eighth: Gambling, drinking alcohol, and drug abuse: 67
Ninth: Consuming the flesh of dead animals, blood, and pork: 67
Tenth: Adultery and sodomy: 67
Eleventh: Consuming usury: 68
Twelfth: Avarice and stinginess: 69
Thirteenth: Lying and false testimony: 69
Fourteenth: Arrogance, self-conceit, self-admiration, and vanity: 70
c. Repentance of prohibited things 71
d. The Muslims' care about the authentic transmission of this religion:...71
The other thing in the science of Hadīth 74
e. A last word: 75

In the Name of Allah, the Most Compassionate, the Most Merciful

Introduction

Praise be to Allah; we praise Him, seek His help, and ask Him for forgiveness. We seek refuge with Allah from the evil of our selves and from our bad deeds. Whoever Allah guides, none can misguide, and whoever He sends astray, none can guide. I testify that there is no god worthy of worship, but Allah and that Muhammad is His slave and Messenger. May Allah's peace and abundant blessings be upon him, his family, and Companions.

To proceed,

There is pressing need today for an abridged and simplified book that presents Islam in its comprehensive sense, in terms of beliefs, acts of worship, dealings, ethics, and the like. It is to help the reader form a clear and complete idea about Islam, and it also serves as an initial reference for new Muslims to learn the rulings, ethics, commands, and prohibitions of this religion. The book should also be handy for the preachers translated into all languages and give it to all those inquiring about Islam and to the new reverts. This way, those whom Allah wills to guide will find guidance, and the argument will be established against the people of misguidance and deviation.

Before starting to write this book, certain courses and regulations should be laid down for the author to abide by. They are meant to help achieve the main objective of this book. Some of these regulations are:

Islam should be presented through the texts of the Noble Qur'an and the purified Sunnah, not through human approaches and scholastic theological methods of debate and argumentation for a number of reasons:

a. By hearing the words of Allah and understanding the intended meanings, those whom Allah wills to guide will be guided and the argument will be established against the astray and the obstinate ones as Allah Almighty says: {If any of the polytheists asks you for protection, give it to him, so that he may hear the Word of Allah, then escort him to his place of safety.}[Surat at-Tawbah: 6] Establishment of the argument and conveyance of the message may not be done properly through human approaches and scholastic theological methods, which are not free from defects and shortcomings.

b. Allah Almighty commanded us to convey His religion and revelation just as it was sent down, and He did not order us to invent scholastic theological ways for guiding people which we think can help us win their hearts. So, why should we preoccupy ourselves with what we are not commanded to do and turn away from what we are commanded to do?

c. With regard to other ways of preaching Islam, like the extensive talk about the opponents' aberrations and refuting their claims, be it in the area of creed, worship, morals, ethics, or economics, or the use of intellectual and mental debates, such as the talk about proving Allah's existence - exalted be He above what the wrongdoers claim - or the talk about the distortions in the Gospel and the Torah, as well as the books of other religions, and revealing their inconsistencies and falsehood, all these can be a way for pointing out the corruption and falsity of the opponents' principles and beliefs, and they can also be a cultural information for Muslims - though there is no harm in not knowing such things. However, these cannot always be a basis for calling people to Allah Almighty.

d. Those who enter Islam on the basis of the approaches mentioned above are not necessarily true Muslims, as some of them may embrace this religion on account of admiring a certain aspect that has been presented to them extensively, even though they do not believe in other major aspects. For example, someone who likes the advantages offered by the Islamic economics but does not believe in the Hereafter or the existence of the jinn and devils, and so on.

People of this type harm Islam more than they benefit it.

e. The Qur'an has such an authority over people's hearts that when we leave it to deal with them uninterrupted, pure souls accept it and get elevated in belief and piety. So, why should any barrier be put between them?

Reactions, the pressure of status quo, and previous backgrounds should not interfere with the presentation of this religion. Rather, it should be presented as it was sent down, while adopting its very approach in addressing people and taking them in a gradual process of uprightness.

Simplicity of style and brevity in writing should be adopted, as much as possible, so that the book can be easily carried and circulate among people.

Let us assume that we finished this work, translated the book, and made ten million copies thereof, which reached the hands of ten million people, and only one percent of them believed in the verses and Hadīths contained therein, coming to us in pursuit of faith, piety, and fear of Allah, whereas 99% disbelieved and turned away. Do you know that this one percent means the entry of a hundred thousand persons into the religion of Islam? This would undoubtedly be a great achievement. If Allah were to guide only one person through you, this would be better for you than possessing the most precious property.

But if none of those invited embraced Islam, and they all rejected it, we have, after all, fulfilled our trust and conveyed the message that our Lord assigned to us.

Indeed, the mission of the Muslim preachers is not to convince people or be keen to guide them, as revealed in the verse that says:**{Even though you are keen to guide them, but Allah does not guide those whom He causes to stray.}**[Surat an-Nahl: 37]Rather, their primary mission is the same as that of their Prophet (may Allah's peace and blessings be upon him) whom Allah Almighty addressed saying:**{O Messenger, convey what has been sent down to you from your Lord. If you do not do that, then**

you have not conveyed His message. Allah will protect you from the people.}[Surat al-Mā'idah: 67]

We implore Allah Almighty to make us all cooperative in the conveyance of His religion to all people and make us callers to goodness and a means leading to it and a cause for blocking every way to evil. Allah knows best and may Allah's peace and blessings be upon our Prophet Muhammad.

Dear reader:

this book introduces Islam to you in a simple way that comprises all its aspects (beliefs, ethics, laws, and all other related teachings).

Meanwhile, I took into consideration several main points:

First: focusing on the fundamentals upon which the religion is

founded. **Second:** adhering to brevity as much as possible.

Third: presenting Islam through its original sources - the Noble Qur'an and the Prophet's Hadīths - so as to leave the reader face to face with the primary sources of this religion from which he can take its guidance and teachings.

As you reach the end of this book, dear reader, you will find that you have gained a clear idea about Islam, after which you can gradually gain more knowledge about this religion.

This book, in your hands, is of interest to a lot of people, as it first and foremost concerns those who desire to embrace Islam and learn its creed, ethics, and rulings.

It also concerns those interested in getting acquainted with religions, especially those religions with hundreds of millions of followers. Moreover, the book concerns the sympathetic friends of Islam who admire some of its traits. It is also intended for the enemies and foes of Islam whose ignorance about this religion may be one of the main reasons behind their hostility and hatred.

Among those greatly concerned about this book are Muslims who want to explain the religion of Islam to people, as this book saves them a lot of effort and makes their mission easier.

If you have no previous idea about Islam, you, O wise reader, may find that you need to read with particular focus and deliberateness so as to grasp the meanings contained in the book. So, do not get bored, for there are numerous Islamic websites where you can get answers to your questions.

1. The word of monotheism (there is no true god but Allah)

The basic rule of Islam is the word of monotheism (there is no true god but Allah). Without this solid rule, the lofty structure of Islam cannot be established. It is the first word to be uttered by anyone entering this religion with belief in all its meanings and connotations. So, what is the meaning of "there is no true god but Allah"?

"There is no true god but Allah" means:

- There is no creator of the universe but Allah.

- There is no owner and disposer of the universe but Allah.

- There is no deity worthy of being worshiped but Allah.

Allah is the One Who created this vast, beautiful, and magnificent universe. This sky and its enormous stars and moving planets, they all move within a perfect system. No one controls them but Allah. And this earth and its mountains, valleys, hills, rivers, trees, plants, air, water, land, and seas, and its day and night, and whoever live and walk thereon are all created and brought into existence by Allah Almighty alone.

In His Noble Book, Allah Almighty says:{**The sun is running to its determined course. That is the design of the All-Mighty, All-Knowing. As for the moon, we have determined phases for it, until it becomes like an old palm stalk. It is not for the sun to catch up with the moon, nor for the night to outstrip the day. Each is floating in its own orbit.**}[Sura Yasīn: 38-40]

{**And We have spread out the earth and set therein firm mountains and caused to grow therein plants of every pleasant kind, as a source of insight and a reminder to every slave who turns [to Allah]. And We send down from the sky blessed rain, with which We cause to grow gardens and grain for harvest, and towering palm trees having clustered fruit.**}[Surat Qāf: 7-10]

This is the creation of Allah, Exalted be He. He made the earth stable and put therein gravity just to the degree needed for life on it. If greater, it would be hard to move; and if lesser, everything would fly. Yet, Allah Almighty created everything with a precise estimate.

And He caused pure water to descend from the sky, which is essential for life on earth.**{We created from water every living thing.}[Surat al-Anbiyā':30]**With such water, He brought forth plants and fruits and quenched the thirst of animals and people. He also enabled the earth to keep the water, which flows therein in streams and rivers.

Moreover, with water He grew gardens that radiate joy stemming from its trees, flowers, and splendor. Indeed, it is Allah Who perfected everything He created and began the creation of man from clay.

The first human being Allah Almighty created was the father of humanity Adam (peace be upon him). He created him from clay and then proportioned and fashioned him and breathed into him from His spirit. Then, He created from him his spouse. Then, He made his progeny out of the extract of a worthless fluid.

Allah Almighty says:**{We created man from an extract of clay, then We placed him as a sperm-drop in a safe place, then We made the sperm-drop into a clinging clot, then We made the clinging clot into a lump, then We made the lump into bones, and We clothed the bones with flesh, and then We developed it into another creation. So Blessed is Allah, the Best of Creators.}[Surat al-Mu'minūn:12-14]**He also says:**{Have you thought about the semen that you emit? Is it you who create it, or is it We Who are the Creators? We have ordained death among you, and nothing can overcome usfrom transforming you and recreating you in forms that you do not know.}[Surat al-Wāqi'ah: 58-61]**Think about your own creation and you will be amazed by these delicate and perfect systems in your body which you only know little about, let alone control. Here is a complete system for digesting food, starting from the mouth where food is cut into small pieces for easy digestion. Then, the piece of food passes through the pharynx (the throat) just to be received by the epiglottis, which allows it to pass to the esophagus and prevents it from passing to the trachea, and then it slides into the stomach through the esophagus that has a worm-like movement. In the stomach, the digestion process continues until the food transforms into a fluid in the stomach passing through the pylorus to the duodenum, where digestion continues, and food turns from its original state into a substance suitable for giving nutrition to the body cells. Then, it goes to the small intestine, where the final phase of digestion is completed, and food turns into such a condition that it can be absorbed by the intestinal villi and circulate with the blood. And there is an integral system particularly designed for blood circulation through such complicated arteries, which if extended, they would be thousands of kilometers long. These are connected to a central pumping station called the heart, which constantly and relentlessly transports the blood through these arteries.

Likewise, there is a system for respiration, and another for the nerves, and another one for the extraction of wastes, and the list goes on. Every day, we gain more knowledge about such systems, yet what we know about ourselves is still far less than what we do not know. So, who could possibly create man in this perfect way but Allah?!

Hence, the greatest sin ever is to set up an equal to Allah while He is the One Who created you.

Proceed with an open heart and a pure soul and ponder over the magnificent creation of the Almighty Lord. This air which you inhale, and it reaches you everywhere, with no color to disturb our vision, if it were cut off from you for only a few minutes, you would die. And this water which you drink, this food that you eat, this person whom you love, and this land on which you walk, and this sky at which you look, all what your eyes can and cannot see, be it small or great, is created by the All-Knowing Creator.

Reflecting upon the creation of Allah leads us to recognize His greatness and power. How foolish, ignorant, and misguided one would be if he sees such splendid, harmonious, and perfect creation, which points to the amazing wisdom and boundless ability, and yet he does not believe in the Creator Who brought all this out of nothing into existence. Allah Almighty says:{**Were they created by none, or were they the creators [of themselves]?Or did they create the heavens and earth? Rather, they are not certain in faith.**}[Surat at-Tūr: 35-36]

Indeed, Allah Almighty is recognized through sound natural dispositions without the need for education. He has put in us the natural need to turn and resort to Him. Yet, some are then made to go astray and away from Him.

That is why when we are hit by a disaster or a severe distress or crisis and face mortal danger in the land or the sea, we immediately turn to Allah for help and rescue; and it is Allah Almighty Who responds to the distressed when they call upon Him and He removes the harm.

This Grand Creator is greater than everything. He cannot be compared to any of His creation, for indeed He is the Great One Whose greatness has not bound, and none can encompass Him in knowledge. He is high above His creation, over His heavens.{**There is nothing like unto Him, and He is the All-Hearing, the All-Seeing.**}[Surat ash-Shūra 11]None in His creation is like Him, and Allah is surely different from whatever comes to our minds. Allah Almighty sees us from above His heavens, but we cannot see Him: {**No vision can encompass Him, but He encompasses all vision, and He is the Most Subtle, the All-Aware.**}[Surat al-An'ām 103]Our senses and powers do not even have the ability by which we can see Him in this worldly life. One of the Prophets asked for this. That was Mūsa (Moses) (peace be upon him) when Allah spoke to him next to Mount Tūr, he said: My Lord, let me look at You. Thereupon, Allah Almighty said to him:{**"You will not be able to see Me. But look at the mountain; if it stays firm in its place, only then will you see Me." When his Lord appeared to the mountain, it was leveled to dust, and Moses fell unconscious. When he recovered, he said, "Glory be to You! I repent to You, and I am the first of the believers."**}[Surat al-A'rāf: 143]The massive mountain fell apart and collapsed as the Almighty Lord revealed Himself to it. So, what about us, human beings, who are very weak?!One of the attributes of Allah Almighty is that He is Able to do all things:**{Allah is not such that something can escape Him in the heavens or on earth.}[Surat Fātir: 44]** Life and death are in His Hand. All creatures stand in need of Him, but He is Self-Sufficient beyond need for anyone. He says:**{O people, it is you who are in need of Allah, whereas Allah is the Self-Sufficient, the Praiseworthy.}[Surat Fātir: 15]** Another attribute of Allah is His knowledge that encompasses all things: **{He alone has the keys of the unseen; no one knows them except Him. He knows what is in the land and sea. Not a leaf falls without His knowledge, nor a grain in the darkness of the earth, nor anything moist or dry, but is [written] in a Clear Record.}[Surat al-An'ām 59]** He knows what we say and what we do and even what we entertain in our hearts:**{He knows the sneaky glances of the eyes and what the hearts conceal.}[Surat Ghāfir: 19]** Allah Almighty is Watching over us and is Aware of our conditions. Nothing in the heavens or earth is hidden from Him, and He is never taken by heedlessness, forgetfulness, or sleep. Allah Almighty says:**{Allah: none has the right to be worshiped except Him, the Ever-Living, All-Sustaining. Neither drowsiness overtakes Him nor sleep. To Him belongs all that is in the heavens and all that is on earth. Who is there that can intercede with Him except with His permission? He knows what was before them and what will be after them, while they encompass nothing of His knowledge, except what He wills. His Kursī [footstool] extends over the heavens and earth, and safeguarding of both does not weary Him, for He is the Highest, the Greatest.}[Surat al-Baqarah: 255]**

To Him belong all attributes of absolute perfection, with no defect or deficiency.

The most beautiful names and the most sublime attributes are His as He says:**{Allah has the Most Beautiful Names, so call upon Him by them, and leave those who profane His Names. They will be recompensed for what they used to do.}[Surat al-A'rāf: 180]**

Allah Almighty has no partner in His dominion and no equal or supporter.

He is far exalted above having a wife or a child. Indeed, He is Self-Sufficient beyond need for all these, as He says:{Say: "He is Allah the One; Allah, the Eternal Refuge. He neither begets nor is He begotten, and there is none comparable to Him."}[Surat al-Ikhlās: 1-4]He also says:{They say, "The Most Compassionate has begotten a son.» You have made a monstrous statement, at which the heavens are about to be torn apart, the earth split asunder, and the mountains tumble down. Because they have ascribed to the Most Compassionate a son. It is not appropriate for the Most Compassionate to beget a son. There is none in the heavens and earth except that he will come to the Most Compassionate in full submission.}[Surat Maryam: 88-93]

Allah Almighty possesses the attributes of majesty, beauty, power, greatness, pride, dominion, and might.

And He also possesses the attributes of generosity, forgiveness, mercy, and benevolence. He is the Most Compassionate, whose mercy encompasses everything.

And He is the Most Merciful, whose mercy precedes His anger.

And He is the Most Generous, whose generosity is boundless and Whose treasures are inexhaustible.

All His names are beautiful, and they point to the attributes of complete perfection that befit none but Allah.

When you know His attributes, you grow in love and glorification for Him, as well as in fear of and submission to Him.

Hence, "there is no true god but Allah" means that nothing of our worship should be devoted to anyone other than Allah. None is worthy of being worshiped except Allah, for He is the One possessing the attributes of divinity and perfection and He is the Creator, the Provider, the Bestower of favors, the One Who gives life and causes death. He alone deserves to be worshiped, with no partner.

If anyone refuses to worship Allah or worships other than Him, he turns to be a polytheist and a disbeliever.

Prostration, bowing, submission, and prayer should be devoted to Allah Almighty alone.

We should seek help only from Allah, supplicate none but Him, seek the fulfillment of our needs only from Him, and avoid dedicating any act of obedience or worship except to Him.{Say, "Indeed, my prayer, my sacrifice, my living and my dying are all for Allah, Lord of the worlds. He has no partner. This is what I have been commanded, and I am the first to submit to Allah."}[Surat al-An'ām: 162-163]

b. Why did Allah create us?

The answer to this key question is of great significance. But it is necessary to get this answer from the divine revelation, for Allah is the One Who created us, and He is the One Who tells us about the purpose of our creation. In the Qur'an, He says:{I have not created the jinn and mankind except to worship Me.}[Surat adh-Dhāriyāt: 56]Servitude to Allah is the common attribute among the countless creatures, from the noblest ones, i.e., the angels, to the strangest creatures. All these nations are naturally disposed to worship and glorify Allah, the Lord of the worlds:{The seven heavens and the earth, and all those in them glorify Him. There is not a single thing that does not glorify Him with His praise, but you do not understand their glorification. Indeed, He is Most Forbearing, All-Forgiving.}[Surat al-Isrā': 44]Angels are made to naturally proclaim Allah's glory just as humans are made to breathe. However, man's servitude to his Creator is voluntary, not compulsory (voluntary by way of testing):{It is He Who created you, yet some of you are disbelievers and some of you are believers. And Allah is All-Seeing of what you do.}[Surat at-Taghābun 2]{Do you not see that to Allah prostrate all those who are in the heavens and all those on earth: the sun, the moon, the stars, the mountains, the trees, the moving creatures, and many humans? But there are many on whom the punishment has become due. Whoever Allah disgraces, none can honor him.}[Surat al-Hajj: 18]Allah has created us to worship Him and to test our success in the fulfillment of this worship. So, whoever worships Allah, loves and submits to Him, and obeys His commands and shuns His prohibitions, he wins His approval, mercy, and love and receives the best reward from Him. Conversely, whoever rejects the worship of Allah, who has created and provided for him, and arrogantly refuses to observe His commands and avoid His prohibitions, he incurs Allah's wrath and faces His painful punishment. Indeed, Allah Almighty did not create us in vain or leave us without a purpose. The most ignorant and foolish are those who come to this world and are endowed with hearing, vision, and mind, and they live for a period of time and then die without knowing why they were brought to this world and where they will go thereafter. Allah Almighty says:**{Did you think that We created you with no purpose, and that you would not be brought back to Us?}**[Surat al-Mu'minūn: 115]

Not equal in His sight are those of us who believe in Him, rely upon Him, refer to Him for judgment, love and submit to Him, and seek closeness to Him through acts of worship and whatever pleases Him and those who disbelieve in Him while He has created and fashioned them, deny His signs and religion, and refuse to submit to His command.

The first type gains honor, reward, love, and pleasure, whereas the other incurs wrath, displeasure, and punishment.

Allah will resurrect people after they die and reward the good doers with bliss and honor in Paradise and punish the evil doers, who arrogantly refused to worship Him, with torment in Hellfire.

You can freely imagine how great this honor and reward will be considering that it will come from Allah, the Self-Sufficient and the Most Generous, whose generosity and mercy are boundless and Whose treasures are inexhaustible. The reward will be the utmost bliss that never ends or goes away (we will talk about this later).

You can likewise imagine how severe and painful the punishment for the disbelievers will be, as it will be inflicted by Allah, the Compeller, the Magnificent, and the Supreme, whose might and pride are boundless.

2. Muhammad is the Messenger of Allah:

Belief in the message of Muhammad (may Allah's peace and blessings be upon him) is the second half of the main pillar of Islam and the mainstay upon which it rests.

One becomes Muslim after he utters the two-part testimony in which he bears witness that there is no true god, but Allah and that Muhammad is the Messenger of Allah.

a. What is the meaning of "messenger"? Who is Muhammad? And were there any messengers other than him?

This is what we will attempt to answer in the coming pages.

A messenger is a man at the peak of truthfulness and noble morals, whom Allah chooses from among people to reveal to him whatever He wishes of the divine commands and matters of the unseen, which he is commanded to convey to people. So, a messenger is a human being, like all other people; he eats and drinks like them and has the same human needs. He, however, is privileged by the revelation coming to him from Allah Almighty through which He informs him of matters of the unseen and the commands of the religion which the messenger is required to convey to people. A messenger is also distinct from other people by the God-given infallibility from falling into major sins or anything that may undermine his mission of conveying the divine message.

We will relate some of the stories of the messengers before Muhammad (may Allah's peace and blessings be upon him) to make it clear that the message of all messengers is the same, namely calling people to worshiping Allah Almighty alone. Let us start with the story of the beginning of humanity and Satan's hostility towards the father of mankind, Adam, and his progeny.

b. The first Messenger was our father Adam (peace be upon him):

Allah Almighty created our father Adam (peace be upon him) out of clay and then breathed from His spirit into him. In this regard, Allah Almighty says:{We surely created you, then shaped you, then We said to the angels, "Prostrate before Adam,"so they prostrated, except Iblīs [Satan], who was not one of those who prostrated. Allah said, "What prevented you from prostrating when I ordered you?"He said, "I am better than him; You created me from fire and created him from clay.» Allah said, "Then get down from here! It is not for you to show arrogance here. Get out, for you are one of the disgraced.» He said, "Grant me respite until the Day they are resurrected.» Allah said, "You are of those who are granted respite".}[Surat al-A'rāf: 11-15]

Satan asked Allah Almighty to give him respite and not subject him to immediate punishment and to allow him to tempt Adam and his posterity out of envy and hatred for them. So, for a wise purpose intended by Allah, He allowed Satan to delude Adam and his progeny except for the sincere servants of Allah, and He commanded Adam and his children not to worship Satan or yield to his temptation and to seek refuge in Allah from him. The first incident of temptation by Satan for Adam and his wife Eve (who was created from his rib) is in the story revealed in the Qur'an:

{"O Adam, dwell in Paradise, you and your wife, and eat from wherever you wish, but do not approach this tree, or else you will both be among the wrongdoers.» Then Satan whispered to them in order to expose what was hidden from them of their private parts. He said, "Your Lord has only forbidden to you this tree to prevent you from becoming angels or immortals.» And he swore to them, "I am indeed your sincere adviser.» So, he deluded them both with deception. When they tasted the tree, their private parts became visible to them, so they began to put together leaves of the Garden to cover themselves. Their Lord called them, "Did I not forbid you from that tree and tell you that Satan is your sworn enemy?» They said, "Our Lord, we have wronged ourselves; if You do not forgive us and have mercy upon us, we will surely be among the losers.» Allah said, "Get down as enemies to one another. You will find a dwelling place on earth and provision for an appointed time.» He said, "There you will live, and there you will die, and from there you will be raised again."O children of Adam we have given you garments that cover your private parts and as an adornment. However, the garment of piety is best. That is one of the signs of Allah, so that they may take heed. O children of Adam, do not let Satan seduce you as he caused your parents to be expelled from the Garden, stripping them of their garments and making their private parts visible to them. He and his offspring see you from where you cannot see them. We have made the devils allies to those who disbelieve.}[Surat al-A'rāf: 19-27]

Adam descended to earth and had children and progeny. Then, he died, and his posterity multiplied generation after generation. They were subject to the devil's temptations and there emerged among them deviation and the worship of the graves of their pious forefathers, and they turned from faith to polytheism. Hence, Allah sent to them a messenger from among themselves, namely Nūh (Noah) (peace be upon him).

c. Noah (peace be upon him):

Ten centuries were between Noah and Adam. Allah Almighty sent him to his people after they had gone astray and turned to the worship of false gods. They used to worship idols, stones, and graves. Among their best-known deities were Wadd, Suwā', Yaghūth, Ya'ūq and Nasr. So, Allah sent him to return them to the worship of Allah alone as revealed in the Qur'an: {Indeed, we sent Noah to his people. He said, "O my people, worship Allah; you have no god other than Him. I fear for you the punishment of a momentous Day."}[Surat al-A'rāf 59] He continued to call his people for a long time, but only a few believed in him. So, he supplicated Allah saying: {He said, "My Lord, I have surely called my people night and day, but my call only drove them further away. Every time I call them so that You may forgive them, they thrust their fingers into their ears and cover their faces with their garments and persist in obstinacy and grow extremely arrogant. Then I called them openly, then I addressed them in public and in private, I said, 'Seek forgiveness from your Lord. Indeed, He is Most Forgiving. He will shower you with abundant rain from the sky, and He will give you wealth and children, and bestow upon you gardens and rivers. What is the matter with you that you do not fear the Majesty of Allah, when He has created you in stages?'"}[Surat Nūh: 5-14]Despite his ongoing effort and amazing keenness to guide his people, they denied and mocked him and accused him of insanity. So, Allah revealed to him that:{None of your people will ever believe except those who have already believed. So do not grieve over what they do.}[Surat Hūd: 36]And He commanded him to build an ark in which he would carry all those who had believed.{So he started constructing the Ark, and every time some chiefs of his people passed by him, they ridiculed him. He said, "If you ridicule us now, we will soon ridicule you as you are ridiculing us. You will come to know who will be afflicted with a disgracing punishment, and upon whom will descend an everlasting punishment. «When Our command came and the oven overflowed, we said, "Take on board a pair from every species and your family – except those who have already been decreed [to drown] – and those who believe." But none believed with him except a few. Noah said, "Board it; in the name of Allah, it sails and anchors. My Lord is All-Forgiving, Most Merciful. «As it sailed with them through waves like mountains, Noah called out to his son, who had kept himself apart, "O my son, come aboard with us, and do not be with the disbelievers. «He said, "I will take shelter on a mountain which will save me from the water." Noah said, "Today no one will be saved from Allah's punishment except those on whom He may have mercy." Thereupon the waves came between them, and he was among those who were drowned. And it was said, "O earth, swallow up your water. O sky, withhold [your rain]!" The water subsided and the command was fulfilled, and the Ark settled on Mount Judi, and it was said, "Away with the wrongdoing people! «Noah called out to his Lord, saying, "My Lord, my son is one of my family, and Your promise is true, and You are the Most Just of all judges! «Allah said,

"O Noah, he is not of your family, for he was not righteous in his conduct. So do not ask Me of what you have no knowledge. I admonish you, so you do not be among the ignorant. Noah said, "My Lord, I seek refuge with You from asking You that of which I have no knowledge. Unless You forgive me and have mercy upon me, I will be among the losers. «It was said, "O Noah, disembark with peace from Us, and with blessings upon you and upon some nations [descending] from those who are with you. As for other nations, we will grant them enjoyment for a while, then they will be afflicted with a painful punishment from Us."}[Surat Hūd: 38]

d. Hūd (peace be upon him):

Sometime later, Allah Almighty sent Hūd (peace be upon him) to the tribe of 'Ād ocated in a region called Al-Ahqāf, after they had gone astray and worshiped false gods.

Allah Almighty informs us about this saying: {To the people of 'Ād We sent their brother Hūd He said, "O my people, worship Allah you have no god other than Him. Will you not then fear Him? «The disbelieving chiefs of his people said, "Indeed, we see you as foolish, and we think that you are one of the liars. «He said, "O my people, there is no foolishness in me, but I am a messenger from the Lord of the worlds, I convey to you the messages of my Lord, and I am your sincere adviser. Are you surprised that a reminder should come to you from your Lord through a man from among yourselves? Remember when He made you successors after the people of Noah and increased you amply in stature. Remember Allah's favors, so that you may be successful. «They said, "Have you come to tell us that we should worship Allah alone and abandon what our forefathers used to worship? Bring upon us what you are threatening us with if you are truthful. «He said, "You are definitely going to be subjected to the punishment and wrath of your Lord. Do you dispute with me concerning mere names that you and your forefathers have made up which Allah has never authorized? Then wait. I am too waiting with you. «Then We saved him and those who were with him by

Our mercy, and exterminated all those who rejected Our signs, for they would not believe.}[Surat al-A'rāf: 65-72]

So, Allah sent upon them a furious wind for the duration of eight days, destroying everything by the command of its Lord, who saved Hūd and the believers with him.

e. Sālih (peace be upon him):

A period of time had passed and there emerged the tribe of Thamūd in the north of the Arabian Peninsula. They turned away from guidance, like those before them. So, Allah sent to them a messenger from among themselves, namely Sālih (peace be upon him), and supported him with a miraculous sign to prove his truthfulness, and that was a great she-camel that had no peer among the creatures. Informing us about his story, Allah Almighty says:{And to the people of Thamūd [We sent] their brother, Sālih. He said, "O my people, worship Allah; you have no god other than Him. There has come to you a clear proof from your Lord: this is a she-camel of Allah, as a sign to you. So, leave her to graze in Allah's land, and do not harm her in any way, or else a painful punishment will seize you. Remember when He made you successors after 'Ād and settled you in the land; you make palaces on its plains and carve homes in the mountains. So, remember the bounties of Allah, and do not spread corruption in the land. «The arrogant chiefs of his people said to those believers who were oppressed, "Do you really know that Sālih has been sent by his Lord?" They said, "We surely believe in what he has been sent with. «Those who were arrogant said, "As for us, we surely disbelieve in what you believe. «Then they killed the she-camel and defied their Lord's command, and said, "Bring us what you threaten us, if you are indeed one of the messengers. «Then an earthquake seized them, and they fell lifeless in their homes. So, he turned away from them, saying, "O my people, I did convey my Lord's message to you and gave you sincere advice, but you do not like sincere advisers."}[Surat al-A'rāf: 73-79]Thereafter, Allah Almighty sent many messengers to the world's communities. All communities received a warner from their Lord.

Allah told us about some of them and did not mention numerous others. They were all sent with one message, namely commanding people to worship Allah alone, with no partner, and to renounce the worship of anyone other than Him. Allah Almighty says:{Indeed, we sent to every community a messenger, [saying], "Worship Allah and shun false gods." Among them were some whom Allah guided, while others were destined to stray. So, travel through the land and see how was the end of the deniers!}[Surat An-Nahl: 36]

f. Ibrāhim (Abraham) (peace be upon him):

Then, Allah Almighty sent Abraham (peace be upon him) to his people after they had gone astray and worshiped the stars and idols. In the Qur'an, He says:{Indeed, we had given Abraham sound judgment before, for We know him well. When he said to his father and his people, "What are these statues to which you are so devoted? «They said, "We found our forefathers worshiping them. «He said, "Indeed, you and your forefathers were clearly misguided. «They said, "Have you come to us with the truth, or are you joking? «He said, "Nay, your Lord is the Lord of the heavens and earth, who created them, and I am one of those who bear witness to it. By Allah, I will surely plot against your idols after you have turned and gone away. «So, he broke them into pieces, except the biggest of them, so that they might come back to it. They said, "Who has done this to our gods? He is indeed one of the wrongdoers. «They said, "We heard a young man, speaking ill of them, who is called Abraham. «They said, "Bring him then before the eyes of the people, so that they may witness [his trial]."They said, "Are you the one who did this to our gods, O Abraham? «He said, "Rather, it was this biggest one who did it. So, ask them, if they can speak! «So, they turned back to one another, ...d. "Indeed, it is you who are the wrongdoers.» Then they turned ...acy, [saying], "You already know that they cannot speak. ... you then worship besides Allah that which can ...ou in the beastie upon you and upon all that ... Do you not have any sense? «They said,

"Burn him and avenge your gods, if you must do something. «We said, "O fire, be cool and safe for Abraham. «They plotted to harm him, but We made them the worst losers.}[Surat al-Anbiyā': 51-70]Then, Abraham and his son Ismā'il (Ishmael) emigrated from Palestine to Makkah, where Allah Almighty commanded them to build the Ka'bah and call upon people to perform Hajj and worship Allah there.{We charged Abraham and Ishmael to purify My House for those who perform circumambulation or stay for worship, or those who bow down and prostrate.}[Surat al-Baqarah: 125]

g. Lūt (Lot) (peace be upon him):

Then, the Almighty Lord sent Lot (peace be upon him) to his evil people, who used to worship other than Allah and engage in immoral acts. Allah Almighty says:{And [We sent] Lot, when he said to his people, "Do you commit such a shameful act that nobody has ever done before you? For you approach men lustfully instead of women; you are but a transgressing people. «The only reply his people gave was to say, "Drive them out of your town, for they are people who keep themselves pure!"}[Surat al-A'rāf: 80-82]So, Allah saved him and his family except for his wife, who was a disbeliever. Allah commanded him to leave the town by night, along with his family. Then, when the command of Allah came, He turned the town upside down and rained upon it stones of layered hard clay.

h. Shu'ayb (peace be upon him):

Then, Allah Almighty sent Shu'ayb (peace be upon him) to the people of Madyan after they had turned away from guidance and after bad morals, including assaulting people and dishonesty in weighing and measuring, had spread amongst them. Informing us about them, our Lord says:{And to the people of Midian [We sent] their brother Shu'ayb. He said, "O my people, worship Allah; you have no god other than Him. There has come to you a clear proof from your Lord. Give full measure and weight, and do not defraud people of their property, and d spread corruption in the land after it has been set aright. That is best for you, if you are [truly] believers. Do not lie in wait on every path, threatening and preventing from Allah's path those who believe in Him, and seeking to make it crooked. Remember when you were few, then He increased you in number. See how was the end of those who spread corruption. If there are some among you who believe in what I have been sent with, while others do not believe, then be patient until Allah judges between us, and He is the Best of Judges. «The arrogant chiefs of his people said, "O Shu'ayb, we will surely drive you and those who believe with you out of our town unless you return to our faith." He said, "Even if we detest it? We would be fabricating lies against Allah if we were to return to your faith after Allah has saved us from it. We will not return to it unless Our Lord Allah so wills. Our Lord has full knowledge of everything. In Allah we put our trust. Our Lord, judge between us and our people with truth, for You are the Best of the Judges. «The disbelieving chiefs of his people said, "If you follow Shu'ayb, you will certainly be losers. «Then they were seized by the earthquake, and they fell lifeless in their homes. Those who rejected Shu'ayb became as if they had never lived there. Those who rejected Shu'ayb were themselves the losers. So, he turned away from them and said, "O my people, I did convey to you the messages of my Lord and gave you sincere advice. Why should I grieve for a disbelieving people?"}[Surat al-A'rāf: 85-93]

i. Mūsa (Moses) (peace be upon him):

There emerged later an arrogant despot in Egypt, called Pharaoh. He claimed to be divine and commanded people to worship him. He used to slaughter and wrong anyone as he wished. Allah Almighty informs us about him saying:{**Indeed, Pharaoh arrogantly elevated himself in the land and divided its people into different factions; oppressing one group of them, slaughtering their sons and sparing their women alive. He was truly one of those who spread corruption. But We wanted to bestow favor upon those who were oppressed in the land and make them leaders and inheritors [of the land],and to establish them in the land,

and to show Pharaoh, Hāmān and their soldiers that which they feared. We inspired the mother of Moses, "Suckle him; but when you fear for him, cast him into the river, and do not fear or grieve. We will surely return him to you and will make him one of the messengers."1Then the household of Pharaoh picked him up, so that he may become an enemy to them and a source of grief. Indeed, Pharaoh, Hāmān and their soldiers were wrongdoers. Pharaoh's wife said, "He is a source of joy for me and you. Do not kill him; he will probably benefit us, or we may adopt him as a son." They were unaware [of the consequences].The heart of Moses' mother became restless; she was about to disclose it, had We not reassured her heart so that she would maintain her faith [in Allah's promise].She said to his sister, "Keep track of him." So, she watched him from a distance, without them noticing. We had already forbidden for him all wet-nurses, then she said, "Shall I direct you to a household who will nurse him for you and take good care of him? «Then We returned him to his mother, so that she would be comforted and not grieve, and so that she would know that Allah's promise is true. Yet most of them do not know. When he reached his full strength and maturity, we gave him wisdom and knowledge. This is how We reward those who do good. Once he entered the city unnoticed by its people and found two men fighting: one of his own people and the other of his enemies. The one from his own people called him for help against his enemy, so Moses struck him with his fist, causing his death. Moses said, "This is of Satan's work; he is a sworn enemy who mislead people. «He said, "My Lord, I have wronged myself, so forgive me," Then He forgave him, for He is indeed the All-Forgiving, the Most Merciful. He said, "My Lord, because of the blessings that You have bestowed upon me, I will never be a supporter to the wicked. «Then he became fearful and vigilant in the city; suddenly the one who sought his help the day before cried out to him again for help. Moses said to him, "You are clearly a troublemaker. «When he was about to strike the one who was an enemy to both of them, he said, "O Moses, do you want to kill me as you killed that person

---

[1] His mother put him in a casket and threw him into the river.

yesterday? You only want to be a tyrant in the land, and you do not want to be one of those who put things right! «Then there came a man rushing from the farthest end of the city, and said, "O Moses, the chiefs are conspiring to kill you, so leave. I am giving you a sincere advice. «So, he left the city, fearful and vigilant. He said, "My Lord, save me from the wrongdoing people. «When he headed towards Midian, he said, "My Lord will surely guide me to a straight way. «When he arrived at the well of Midian, he found a crowd of people watering [their flocks] and found apart from them two women holding [their flocks] back. He said, "What is the matter with you?" They said, "We cannot water [them] until the shepherds take [their flocks] away, and our father is a very old man."So he watered [their flocks] for them, then he turned to the shade and said, "My Lord, I am desperately in need of whatever good You may send down to me."Then one of the two women came to him, walking modestly. She said, "My father is inviting you so that he may reward you for watering [our flocks] for us." When he came to him and told him the whole story, he said, "Have no fear. You are now safe from the wrongdoing people. «One of the two daughters said, "O dear father, hire him; the best one you can hire is the strong and trustworthy. «He said, "I would like to give you one of these two daughters of mine in marriage, provided that you serve me for eight years; if you complete ten, it will be of your own free will. I do not want to make things difficult for you. You will find me, if Allah wills, from among the righteous. «Moses said, "Let that be the agreement between me and you. Whichever of the two terms I complete, there will be no further obligation on me, and Allah is Witness over what we say. «When Moses had completed the term and was traveling with his family, he spotted a fire in the direction of Mount Tūr. He said to his family, "Stay here; I have spotted a fire. Perhaps I will bring you from there some news or a brand of fire so that you may warm yourselves. «But when he came to it, he was called from the tree in the sacred ground on the right side of the valley: "O Moses, I am Allah, the Lord of the worlds. Throw down your staff." But when he saw it slithering as if it were a snake, he turned and ran away without looking back. [Allah said], "O Moses, come back, and have no fear; you are perfectly safe. Put your hand into your garment, it will come out shining white without blemish; and draw your arms tight to you to calm your fear. These are two proofs from your Lord to Pharaoh and his chiefs, for they are indeed a rebellious people. «Moses said, "My Lord, I have killed one of their men, and I fear that they may kill me. My brother Aaron is more eloquent than me in speech, so send him with me as a helper to confirm my words, for I fear that they may reject me." Allah said, "We will strengthen you through your brother and give you both power, so they cannot harm you. With Our signs, you and your followers will prevail."}[Surat al-Qasas: 4-35]

Moses and his brother Hārūn (Aaron) went to Pharaoh, the arrogant king, and called him to worship Allah, the Lord of the worlds:{Pharaoh said, "What is 'the Lord of the worlds'? «Moses said, "The Lord of the heavens and earth and all that is between them, if only you had sure faith. «Pharaoh said to those around him, "Did you hear [what he just said]?"Moses said, "Your Lord and the Lord of your forefathers. «Pharaoh said, "Your messenger who has been sent to you is truly insane! «Moses said, "Lord of the east and west and all that is between them, if only you had sense! «Pharaoh said, "If you take any god other than me, I will throw you into prison. «Moses said, "What if I bring you a clear proof? «Pharaoh said, "Bring it then, if you are truthful! «So, he threw down his staff, and suddenly it was a real serpent. And he drew out his hand, and it was glowing white to the beholders. Pharaoh said to the chiefs around him, "This is indeed a learned magician! He wants to drive you out of your land with his magic. What do you suggest? «They said, "Let him and his brother wait and dispatch heralds to the citiesto bring you every learned magician. «So, the magicians were assembled at an appointed time on a known day. And it was said to the people, "Will you join the gathering, so that we may follow the magicians if they are victorious? «When the magicians came, they said to Pharaoh, "Will there be a reward for us if we are victorious? «He said, "Yes, and then you will surely be of those who are close to me."Moses said to them, "Throw whatever you wish to throw. «So, they threw their ropes and staffs, and said, "By the glory of Pharaoh, it is we who will be the victorious! «Then Moses threw his staff, and at once it swallowed up all objects of their illusion. So, the magicians fell down in prostration. They said, "We believe in the Lord of the worlds, the Lord of Moses and Aaron. «Pharaoh said, "How dare you believe in him before I give you permission. Indeed, he is your master who taught you magic, but you will soon come to know. I will surely cut off your hands and feet on opposite sides, then I will crucify you all. «They said, "No harm; we will surely return to our Lord. We hope that our Lord will forgive us our sins, as we are the first of the believers. «We inspired Moses, "Leave with My slaves by night; you will surely be pursued. «So, Pharaoh sent heralds to the cities, saying, "These are but a small band, and they have enraged us, but we are all well-prepared. «Thus, did We drive them out of their gardens and springs, and their treasures and splendid dwellings. So it was; and We made the Children of Israel to inherit them. They pursued them at sunrise. When the two groups saw each other, the companions of Moses said, "We are surely overtaken! «Moses said, "Certainly not! My Lord is with me; He will guide me."Then We inspired Moses, "Strike the sea with your staff," so it parted, each part became like a huge mountain. Then We brought the others [pursuers] close to that place, and We saved Moses and all those who were with him, then We drowned the others. Indeed, there is a sign in this, yet most of them would not believe. Indeed, your Lord is the All-Mighty, the Most Merciful.}[Surat ash-Shu'arā': 23-68]When Pharaoh was about to drown, he said: I believe that there is no god but the One in Whom the children of Israel believe. Thereupon, Allah Almighty says:{Now [you believe]? You had always been disobedient and were one of the mischief-makers! So today We will preserve your body, so that you will be an example for those who come after you, yet most people are heedless of Our signs.} [Surat Yūnus: 91-92]

Then, Allah made the people of Moses, who had been wronged, inheritors of the eastern and western parts of earth which Allah blessed, and He destroyed what Pharaoh and his people had done.

Allah then revealed to Moses the Torah, a book containing guidance for people and light to lead them to what Allah loves and what pleases Him and elucidating the lawful and unlawful to be observed by the children of Israel (the people of Moses).

After Moses (peace be upon him) had passed away, Allah Almighty sent numerous prophets to his people - the children of Israel - guiding them to the right path. Whenever a prophet died, another would succeed him.

Allah Almighty mentioned to us some of these prophets, such as Dāwūd (David), Sulaymān (Solomon), Ayyūb (Job), and Zakariya (Zechariah), and many others were not mentioned. Then, He sealed those prophets with 'Isa (Jesus), the son of Mary, whose life abounded with miraculous signs, starting with his birth and ending with his ascension to heaven.

The Torah, revealed by Allah Almighty to Moses, went through distortions and alterations over time at the hands of the Jews, who alleged to be the followers of Moses, while Moses is disassociated from them. The Torah they hold now is no longer the Book that Allah sent down, as they added thereto things not appropriate to come from the Creator and ascribed to Allah therein attributes of deficiency, ignorance, and weakness, far exalted be Allah above what they say. Allah Almighty says describing them:{**So woe to those who write the Scripture with their own hands, and then say, "This is from Allah," in order to trade it for a small price. Woe to them for what their hands have written, and woe to them for what they earn.**}[Surat al-Baqarah: 79]

j. 'Isa (Jesus) (peace be upon him):

Maryam (Mary), the chaste pure daughter of 'Imrān, was a devoted worshiper who adhered to the commands of Allah that had been revealed to the prophets after Moses. She was a member of the family which Allah Almighty chose above all humankind. In the Qur'an, Allah says:{**Allah chose Adam and Noah, the family of Abraham, and the family of 'Imrān above all people.**}[Surat Āl 'Imrān: 33]The angels gave her glad tidings that Allah had chosen her:{And [remember] when the angels said, "O Mary, Allah has chosen you, purified you, and chosen you over all women.O Mary, worship your Lord devoutly, prostrate yourself and bow down with those who bow down."}[Surat Āl 'Imrān: 42-43]Then, Allah Almighty informs how He created Jesus in her womb without a father. He says:{And mention in the Book [the story of] Mary when she withdrew from her family to a place towards the east. She screened herself from them, then We sent to her Our Spirit [Gabriel] and he appeared before her in the form of a perfect human being. She said, "I seek refuge in the Most Compassionate from you; [do not approach me] if you fear Allah. «He said, "I am only a messenger from your Lord to grant you a righteous son. «She said, "How can I have a son when no man has touched me, nor have I ever been unchaste? «He said, "Thus it will be your Lord says, 'It is easy for Me; We make him a sign for people and a mercy from Us. This matter has already been decreed.' «So, she conceived him and withdrew with him to a distant place. The pains of labor drove her to the trunk of a palm tree. She said, "Oh, would that I had died before this and had been completely forgotten! «Then the baby called her from beneath her, "Do not grieve; your Lord has provided a stream beneath you. Shake the trunk of the palm tree towards yourself; fresh ripe dates will drop upon you. Eat and drink and be glad. And if you see any human being, say, 'I have vowed silence to the Most Compassionate, so I will not talk to any human being today.' «Then she came to her people carrying him. They said, "O Mary, you have committed something monstrous sister of Aaron, your father was not a man of evil, nor was your mother unchaste. «Thereupon she pointed to him. They said, "How can we talk to someone who is still a baby in the cradle? Jesus said, "I am a slave of Allah. He has given me the Scripture and made me a prophet. He has made me blessed wherever I may be and has enjoined upon me prayer and Zakah as long as I am alive, and has made me dutiful to my mother, and has not made me an oppressor or disobedient. Peace is upon me the day I was born, the day I will die and the day I will be resurrected. «Such was Jesus, son of Mary – a word of truth about which they are in doubt. It is not befitting Allah to beget a son. Glory be to Him! When He decrees a matter, He only says to it, "Be," and it is.[Jesus said], "Indeed, Allah is my Lord and your Lord, so worship Him. This is a straight path."}[Surat Maryam: 16-36]When Jesus (peace be upon him) called people to the worship of Allah, some accepted his call, but many rejected it. He kept calling them to worship Allah and faced disbelief and hostility from a lot of the people, who even tried to kill him. Thereupon, Allah said to him **{Jesus, I will take you and raise you up to Myself and deliver you from those who disbelieve.}[Surat Āl 'Imrān: 55]**Allah Almighty made one of those pursuing him look like him. So, people seized that person mistaking him for Jesus (peace be upon him), and they killed and crucified him. As for Jesus, son of Mary, Allah raised him to Himself. Before his departure, he informed his disciples that Allah would send another messenger called Ahmad to convey and spread the religion. A Qur'anic verse reads:**{And [remember] when Jesus, son of Mary, said, "O Children of Israel, I am truly a messenger of Allah to you, confirming the Torah which came before me, and giving glad tidings of a messenger after me whose name will be Ahmad."}[Surat as-Saff: 6]**After a period of time, the followers of Jesus were divided and there emerged a sect that went to extremes with regard to him, claiming that he is the son of Allah, far exalted is Allah above their claim. They were tempted in this claim by the fact that Jesus (peace be upon him) had been born without a father. In this regard, Allah Almighty says:**{The similitude of Jesus before Allah is like that of Adam; He created him from dust, then said to him, "Be," and he was.}[Surat Āl 'Imrān: 59]**Indeed, the creation of Jesus without a father is not more amazing than the creation of Adam with no father or mother. Hence, Allah Almighty addresses the Children of Israel in the Qur'an and commands them to keep away from this disbelief saying:**{O People of the Book, do not go to extremes in your religion, and do not say about Allah but the truth. The Messiah, Jesus, son of Mary, was only a messenger of Allah, and His Word that He bestowed upon Mary, and a spirit from Him. So, believe in Allah and His messengers and do not say "Three" [Trinity]. Cease: that is better for you. Indeed, Allah is the only One God. Glory be to Him, [far exalted is He] to have a son. To Him belongs all that is in the heavens and all that is on earth, and sufficient is Allah as a Disposer of**

Affairs. The Messiah would never disdain to be a slave of Allah, nor would the nearest angels to Him. Those who disdain to worship Him and are arrogant, He will gather them all together before Him. As for those who believe and do righteous deeds, He will give them their rewards in full and will increase them out of His bounty. But those who disdain and act arrogantly, He will subject them to a painful punishment, and they will not find for themselves any protector or helper besides Allah.}[Surat an-Nisā': 171-173]Addressing Jesus on the Day of Judgment, Allah Almighty says:{When Allah will say, "O Jesus, son of Mary, did you tell people, 'Take me and my mother as gods besides Allah?'" He will say, "Glory be to You! It is not for me to say what I have no right. Had I said so, you would have surely known it. You know what is within myself, whereas I do not know what is within Yourself. Indeed, you are the All-Knower of all unseen. I did not tell them except what You ordered me – 'Worship Allah, my Lord and your Lord.' I was witness over them as long as I was among them. But when You took me up, You Yourself were Watcher over them, and You are a Witness over all things. If You punish them, they are Your slaves; if You forgive them, you are indeed the All-Mighty, the All-Wise. «Allah will say, "This is the Day when the truthfulness of the truthful will benefit them; they will have gardens under which rivers flow, abiding therein forever. Allah is pleased with them, and they are pleased with Him. That is the supreme triumph."} [Surat al-Mā'idah: 116-119]

Hence, the Messiah Jesus, the son of Mary, is innocent of these millions who call themselves Christians and believe they are followers of Jesus Christ.

3. Muhammad, the Messenger of Allah (the seal of prophets and messengers)

Nearly six centuries passed after Jesus (peace be upon him) had been raised to heaven, during which people swerved from guidance and turned to disbelief and error and worshiped others besides Allah. So, Allah Almighty sent Muhammad (may Allah's peace and blessings be upon him) in Makkah, Hijaz, with guidance and the true religion, calling people to worship Allah alone, with no partner. He supported him with signs and miracles that proved his prophethood and message. He made him the seal of the messengers and made his religion the final one, preserving it from distortions and alterations till the end of time. So, who is Muhammad? Who are his people? How did Allah send him? What are the signs of his prophethood? What are the details of his life and biography? This is what we will attempt to present and clarify in these few pages.

a. His lineage and honor

He is Muhammad ibn 'Abdullah ibn 'Abd al-Muttalib ibn Hāshim ibn 'Abd Manāt ibn Qusayy ibn Kilāb. His lineage goes back to Ishmael the son of Abraham (peace be upon both of them), from Quraysh, an Arab tribe. He was born in Makkah in 571 AD. His father died while he was still in his mother's womb. So, he grew up as an orphan under the care of his grandfather 'Abd al-Muttalib and later, after his grandfather's death, under the care of his paternal uncle Abu Tālib.

b. His traits

We have previously noted that a messenger chosen by Allah Almighty should be at the climax of purity, truthfulness, and noble morals, and that was the exact description of Muhammad (may Allah's peace and blessings be upon him). He grew up as a truthful and honest man, known for his good morals, kind speech, and eloquence. He was loved by everyone, near and far, and was held in high esteem among his people. They called him "the honest one" and would entrust him with their precious possessions whenever they went on a journey.

In addition to his good morals, he was also of a good appearance. The eyes would always enjoy looking at him. He had a white face, wide eyes, long eyelashes, black hair, broad shoulders, and moderate height, closer to being tall. One of the Companions described him saying: «I saw the Messenger of Allah (may Allah's peace and blessings be upon him) in a Yemeni garment, and I had never seen anyone better looking than him. «He was unlettered, who could not read or write, and lived among mostly unlettered people. Few of them would read and write. They, however, were smart, quick-witted, and with sharp memory.

c. Quraysh and the Arabs

The Prophet's people and clan lived in Makkah beside the Ka'bah, which Allah Almighty had commanded Abraham and his son Ishmael (peace be upon them) to build.

As many years passed, they deviated from the religion of Abraham - sincere worship of Allah alone - and, along with the surrounding tribes, they placed idols of stones, trees, and gold around the Ka'bah. They deemed them sacred and believed that they could bring about benefit and cause harm. Moreover, they created certain rituals in worship to these idols, the biggest and the most important and famous of which was the one called Hubal. There were other idols and trees outside Makkah, worshiped apart from Allah and held in sanctity, like Al-Lāt, Al-'Uzza, and Manāt. The relationship between different tribes was marked by arrogance, pride, aggression, and grinding wars. They, nonetheless, had some good traits like bravery, hospitality, and truthfulness.

d. The start of the Prophet's mission

At the age of forty, and one day when the Prophet (may Allah's peace and blessings be upon him) was in the cave of Hirā' outside Makkah, he received the first revelation from heaven through Angel Jibrīl (Gabriel) who pressed him and said: "Read!" He said: "I cannot read." He again pressed him strongly and repeated the request and received the same reply. He did this for a third time, pressing him more strongly and asking him to read, and the reply was: "What should I read?" Thereupon, he said:{**Read in the name of your Lord Who created, created man from a clinging clot. Read, and your Lord is the Most Generous, who taught by the pen, taught man what he did not know.**}[Surat al-'Alaq: 1-5]

The angel went off and left him. So, the Prophet (may Allah's peace and blessings be upon him) returned to his house and wife, in fear and panic. He said to his wife Khadījah: "Cover me, for I fear for myself." She said: "No, by Allah, Allah will never humiliate you for you maintain kinship ties, help the poor, and assist those hit by calamities."

Then, Gabriel came to him in the form Allah had created him in, blocking the horizon. He said: "O Muhammad, I am Gabriel, and you are the Messenger of Allah."

Thereafter, the revelation successively came from heaven, commanding the Messenger of Allah (may Allah's peace and blessings be upon him) to call his people to worship Allah alone and to warn them of polytheism and disbelief. So, he began to call his people, one by one, starting from the nearest ones, to embrace Islam. The first to believe in him were his wife Khadījah bint Khuwaylid, his friend Abu Bakr as-Siddīq, and his cousin 'Ali ibn Abi Tālib.

As his people knew about his call, they began to confront him and plot against him. One morning, he came out and called out loud: "O morning!" A word used at that time for the purpose of gathering people. The people gathered one after another to hear what he had to say. When they gathered, he said to them: "What if I informed you that the enemy would attack you in the morning or in the evening - would you believe me?" They said: "We have never seen you lying." He said: "Indeed, I am a warner to you, ahead of a severe punishment." Thereupon, his paternal uncle Abu Lahab said to him: "May you perish, is it for this that you have gathered us?!" So, Allah Almighty revealed:{**May the hands of Abu Lahab perish,** and may he perish! Neither his wealth nor his worldly gains will avail him. He will burn in a Flaming Fire, and so will his wife, the carrier of firewood, around her neck will be a rope of palm fiber.}[Surat al-Masad: 1-5]

The Prophet (may Allah's peace and blessings be upon him) kept calling them to Islam and asking them, "say: 'There is no god but Allah', only then you will succeed." But they said: "Has he made gods only one god? This is strange indeed."

Allah Almighty revealed verses that called them to guidance and warned them of the error they were in. Some of these verses read:{Say, "Do you disbelieve in the One Who created the earth in two Days, and you set up rivals to Him? Such is the Lord of the worlds. He placed on it firm mountains standing high above it, and showered His blessings upon it, and measured its sustenance totaling exactly four Days, for all who ask. Then He turned to the heaven when it was all smoke, and said to it and to the earth, 'Come into being, willingly or unwillingly.' They both said, 'We come willingly. 'He then formed them into seven heavens in two Days and assigned to each heaven its mandate. And We adorned the lowest heaven with lamps [stars] which also serve as a protection. That is the design of the All-Mighty, the All-Knowing. «But if they turn away, then say, "I warn you of a blast like the one that befell 'Ād and Thamūd."}[Surat Fussilat: 9-13]

However, these verses and this call only increased them in obstinacy and arrogant rejection of the truth. They even began to inflict harsh torment upon anyone accepting Islam, especially the weak ones who had no means of protection. They would, for example, place a large rock upon the chest of one of them and drag him through the markets during severe heat, ordering him to disbelieve in the religion of Muhammad or remain in this torment. Many of them died from severe torture.

As for the Prophet (may Allah's peace and blessings be upon him), he enjoyed the protection of his paternal uncle Abu Tālib, who loved and sympathized with him. He was a respected leader in Quraysh; however, he did not embrace Islam.

Quraysh tried to strike a deal with the Messenger of Allah (may Allah's peace and blessings be upon him). They offered him money, authority, and other temptations provided that he should give up the call to this new religion, which insulted the idols they sanctified and worshiped apart from Allah. In response, the Prophet (may Allah's peace and blessings be upon him) displayed a firm and categorical stance, for this was a message that Allah commanded him to convey to people, and were he to disobey the command, Allah would punish him. He told them that he wanted good for them, and they were his people and kith and kin. «By Allah, if I were to lie to all people, I would not lie to you, and if I were to deceive all people, I would not deceive you."

When their attempts to strike a deal to stop his call to Allah bore no fruit, the Quraysh became more hostile towards the Prophet (may Allah's peace and blessings be upon him) and his followers. They asked Abu Tālib to hand Muhammad over to them so that they would kill him, in return for whatever he wanted, or otherwise he should stop proclaiming his religion amongst them. So, his uncle asked him to cease his call to this religion.

Feeling sad, the Prophet (may Allah's peace and blessings be upon him) said: «By Allah, O uncle, if they were to place the sun in my right hand and the moon in my left hand so that I should give up this religion, I would not give it up until Allah makes it dominant or I perish in the process. «Thereupon, his uncle said: "Go ahead and say whatever you wish. By Allah, they would not be able to harm you in any way before I die in defending you". Later, as Abu Tālib was dying, and some leading tribesmen were present, the Messenger of Allah (may Allah's peace and blessings be upon him) came and was requesting him eagerly to embrace Islam, saying: "Uncle, say a word by which I can intercede for you with Allah. Say: There is no god but Allah". Witnessing that, the notables said: "Would you renounce the religion of 'Abd al-Muttalib (would you renounce of the religion of your forefathers)?" So, he found it too grave that he should leave the religion of his forefathers and enter Islam. Hence, he died as a polytheist. The Prophet (may Allah's peace and blessings be upon him) grieved so much because his uncle died as a polytheist. So, Allah Almighty addressed him saying:{**You cannot guide whoever you like, but Allah guides whom He wills, and He knows best who will be guided.**}[Surat al-Qasas: 56]

After his uncle's death, the Prophet (may Allah's peace and blessings be upon him) suffered harm. They would place filth (taken from animals) over his back while he was praying at the Ka'bah.

Thereafter, the Prophet (may Allah's peace and blessings be upon him) headed to Taif, 70 km from Makkah, to call its people to Islam. They, however, opposed his call more vehemently than the people of Makkah and incited their fools to throw stones at the Prophet (may Allah's peace and blessings be upon him) as they expelled him from their town. They followed him with stones and injured his honored heels.

In that state, the Prophet (may Allah's peace and blessings be upon him) turned to his Lord in supplication and pursuit of support. So, Allah Almighty sent him the angel telling him that his Lord had heard the people's reaction to him, and he would cause the two large mountains to crash upon them, if he so willed. He replied: "No, but I hope that Allah would bring out of their children those who would worship Allah alone and associate none with Him".

Then, the Prophet (may Allah's peace and blessings be upon him) returned to Makkah, where the hostility continued towards all those who believed in him. Later, a delegation from Yathrib - which was then called Madīnah - came to him, and he invited them to Islam. They embraced Islam. So, he sent with them one of his Companions, called Mus'ab ibn 'Umayr, to teach them Islam. Many from the people of Madīnah accepted Islam at his hand.

The following year, they came back to the Prophet (may Allah's peace and blessings be upon him) to give him the pledge of allegiance on Islam.

Then, he instructed his persecuted Companions to emigrate to Madīnah, which they did, individually and in groups. They were, thus, called "Al-Muhājirūn" (the Immigrants). The people of Madīnah welcomed and honored them and shared with them their houses and properties. Hence, they were later called "Al-Ansār" (the Supporters).

When Quraysh learned about this Hijrah (immigration), they were determined to kill the Prophet (may Allah's peace and blessings be upon him). Hence, they planned to besiege the house where he passed the night and to strike him collectively with the sword on coming out. Allah Almighty saved him, however, and he came out while they were unaware. Then, Abu Bakr as-Siddīq caught up with him and he instructed 'Ali to stay in Makkah to return the trusts left with the Prophet (may Allah's peace and blessings be upon him) to their owners.

While the Prophet (may Allah's peace and blessings be upon him) was on the path of Hijrah, Quraysh declared a huge prize for whoever could seize Muhammad (may Allah's peace and blessings be upon him) alive or dead. But Allah Almighty saved him and made him and his Companion reach Madīnah safe and sound.

The people of Madīnah received him in a welcoming, cheerful, and an extremely joyful manner. They all came out to meet him, chanting: The Messenger of Allah has come; the Messenger of Allah has come.

The Prophet (may Allah's peace and blessings be upon him) settled in Madīnah. The first thing he did was constructing a mosque, where the prayer would be performed. He began to teach people the laws of Islam and noble morals and to recite the Qur'an to them. His Companions rallied around him, taking guidance from him, purifying their souls, and refining their manners. Their love for the Prophet (may Allah's peace and blessings be upon him) deepened and they got influenced by his sublime attributes; and the brotherly bond of faith strengthened among them. Madinah truly became a utopia that lived in an atmosphere of happiness and brotherliness, with no difference between rich and poor, black and white, and Arab and non-Arab. The only criterion of distinction was faith and piety. Out of this elite community, the best generation that history has ever known emerged.

One year after the Prophet's Hijrah, confrontations and battles began between the Messenger of Allah along with his Companions against Quraysh and its allies who were hostile towards Islam.

The first battle between the two sides, the Great Battle of Badr, took place in a valley located between Makkah and Madīnah. Allah Almighty supported the Muslims, 314 fighters, against Quraysh, one thousand fighters. The Muslims attained a clear victory, killing seventy of the Quraysh fighters, most of them were leaders and senior figures, and taking seventy captives, while the rest ran away.

There followed other battles between the Messenger of Allah (may Allah's peace and blessings be upon him) and Quraysh, in the last of which (8 years after his leaving Makkah) he managed to lead an army of ten thousand Muslim fighters towards Makkah to attack Quraysh on their own grounds and inflict a crushing defeat on them. He overcame his tribe that had sought to kill him, tortured his Companions, and prevented people from the religion that Allah sent down to him.

Following this remarkable victory, he gathered them and said:**"O people of Quraysh, what do you think I will do to you?"** They said: "You are a noble brother and the son of a noble brother." He said: **"Go, for you are set free."** He pardoned them and gave them the free choice to embrace Islam.

This prompted people to enter the religion of Islam in multitudes, and then the entire Arabian Peninsula embraced Islam.

Shortly afterwards, the Prophet (may Allah's peace and blessings be upon him) performed Hajj along with 114000 who had recently embraced Islam.

On the day of 'Arafah, he stood and delivered a sermon in which he clarified the rulings and laws of Islam. Then, he remarked: "I may not meet you after this year. Behold! Those present should convey this to those who are absent." Then, he looked at them and said: "Have I conveyed the message?" The people replied: "Yes." He said: "O Allah, bear witness." He again said: "Have I conveyed the message." The people replied in the affirmative, and he said: "O Allah, bear witness."

After Hajj, the Prophet (may Allah's peace and blessings be upon him) returned to Madīnah and one day he addressed people saying that Allah Almighty gave someone a choice between living eternally and what is with Allah, and he chose what is with Allah. The Companions wept, knowing that he had meant himself and that his departure from this world was imminent. On Monday, the 12th of Rabī' al-Awwal, 11 AH, the Prophet's illness worsened, and he started suffering the throes of death. He gave a farewell look at his Companions and exhorted them to adhere to performing the prayer. Then he breathed his last and departed to the Supreme Companion.

The Companions were extremely shocked and sad for his death to the extent that one of them - 'Umar ibn al-Khattāb (may Allah be pleased with him) - unsheathed his sword and threatened to kill anyone saying that the Prophet (may Allah's peace and blessings be upon him) had died.

Thereupon, Abu Bakr came and reminded him of the verse saying: **{Muhammad is no more than a messenger; there were messengers passed away before him. If he dies or is killed, will you turn back on your heels? Anyone who turns back on his heels will not harm Allah in the least, but Allah will reward those who are grateful.}**[Surat Āl 'Imrān: 144]Upon hearing this verse, 'Umar fell unconscious.

This is Muhammad, the Messenger of Allah, the seal of all prophets and messengers. Allah sent him to all mankind as a warner and bringer of glad tidings. And he conveyed the message, fulfilled the trust, and gave sincere advice to the Ummah.

Allah Almighty supported him with the Noble Qur'an, the divine revealed speech that**{No falsehood can approach it from the front or**

from behind; a revelation from the One Who is All-Wise, Praiseworthy.}[Surat Fussilat: 42] If all people, from the beginning of humanity to the end of times, were to gather and jointly try to produce something like the Qur'an, they would not be able to, even if they collaborated with one another. Allah Almighty says:**{O mankind, worship your Lord, who created you and those before you, so that you may become righteous; He Who made the earth a resting-place for you, and the sky a canopy; and sends down rain from the sky, and brings forth fruits thereby as a provision for you. So do not set up rivals to Allah while you know. If you are in doubt concerning that which We have sent down upon Our slave, then produce a chapter like it and call upon your helpers other than Allah, if you are truthful. But if you did not do it, and you can never do it; then beware of the Fire whose fuel will be people and stones, which is prepared for the disbelievers. And give glad tidings to those who believe and do righteous deeds that they will have gardens under which rivers flow. Every time they are provided with a provision of fruit therefrom, they will say, "This is what we were provided with before," for they will be given fruit that resemble one another. They will have purified spouses, and they will abide therein forever.}[Surat al-Baqarah: 21-25]**

The Qur'an consists of 114 surahs, which comprise over six thousand verses. Allah Almighty challenges people over all ages to produce one surah similar to its surahs, knowing that the shortest surah in the Qur'an consists of three verses only.

If they could do so, they would then know that this Qur'an did not come from Allah. Indeed, this is one of the greatest miracles by which Allah supported His Messenger. He also supported him with other miracles and supernatural acts, such as the following:

e. Supporting the Prophet with miracles:

1. He would supplicate Allah and place his hand in a vessel, and as a result, water would spring forth from between his fingers. The whole army, more than a thousand, would drink from this water.

2. He would supplicate Allah and place his hand in food, which would increase in the bowl and suffice 1500 Companions.

3. He would raise his hands towards the sky in supplication for rain and before leaving his place, drops of water would fall down his face from rain, and other numerous miracles.

Allah Almighty also supported him with His protection. None of those seeking to kill him would ever be able to reach him and extinguish the light that he came with from Allah. In the Qur'an, Allah says:{**O Messenger, convey what has been sent down to you from your Lord. If you do not do that, then you have not conveyed His message. Allah will protect you from the people...**}[Surat al-Mā'idah: 67]Despite Allah's support for him, the Prophet (may Allah's peace and blessings be upon him) was still a role model in all his words and deeds, and he was the first to obey the divine commands revealed to him, the most keen on performing the acts of worship and obedience, and the most generous, readily spending in charity whatever he had, giving it to the poor and needy - even the inheritance as he once said: "We, the prophets, do not leave inheritance. Whatever we leave is charity". 2

As for his morals, they are higher than anyone could ever reach. Everyone who accompanied him would love him from the bottom of his

---

[2] Narrated by Ahmad (2/463) with an authentic Isnād] A similar Hadīth, which was mentioned by Ahmad Shākir in his review of "Musnad" (19/92), reads: "My heirs will not inherit a dinar, for whatever I leave, excluding the adequate support of my wives the wage of a worker, is to be given in charity."

heart, and the Prophet would become dearer to him than his children, parents, and all people.

Anas ibn Mālik, the Prophet's servant, said: "I never touched a hand that is better, softer, or more fragrant than the hand of the Messenger of Allah. I served him for ten years, and he never said to me: 'Why did you do that?' for something I had done, nor did he ever say to me: 'Why did you not do that?' for something I had not done." [3]

This is Muhammad the Messenger of Allah. Our Lord raised his status and reputation among all humankind. No one is mentioned today in the whole world as often as he is mentioned. Since 1400 years, millions of minarets all over the globe announce the Adhān (call to prayer) five times a day and proclaim: "I bear witness that Muhammad is the Messenger of Allah". And millions of worshipers repeat the same phrase tens of times every day in their prayers: "I bear witness that Muhammad is the Messenger of Allah".

f. The noble Companions

After the Prophet's death, his noble Companions shouldered the responsibility of the call to Islam and dispersed far and wide to spread it. They were, indeed, the best callers to this religion. Of all people, they were the most truthful in speech, the most just, and the most honest, and they had the greatest interest in guiding people and spreading goodness among them.

They assumed the morals and traits of the prophets. So, their morals played a remarkable role in people's acceptance of this religion in different parts of the world. They willingly embraced Islam in large numbers, from West Africa to East Asia and Central Europe, without any coercion.

---

[3] Narrated by Al-Bukhāri (4/230)

These are the Companions of the Messenger of Allah, the best people after the prophets. The most famous among them are the four rightly guided Caliphs, who ruled the Muslim state after the Prophet's death. They are:

1. Abu Bakr as-Siddīq.

2. 'Umar ibn al-Khattāb.

3. 'Uthmān ibn 'Affān.

4. 'Ali ibn Abi Tālib.

Muslims hold feelings of recognition and appreciation towards them and draw close to Allah Almighty by loving His Messenger and his Companions, men and women, respecting and revering them.

No one would hate or insult them except a disbeliever in Islam, even if he claims to be a Muslim. Allah Almighty praises them saying:{**You are the best nation ever raised for mankind: you enjoin what is right and forbid what is wrong, and believe in Allah.**}[Surat Āl-Imrān: 110] And He affirmed His pleasure with them when they gave the pledge of allegiance to the Prophet (may Allah's peace and blessings be upon him) as He says: {**Indeed, Allah was pleased with the believers when they pledged allegiance to you [O Prophet] under the tree. He knew what was in their hearts, so He sent down tranquility upon them and rewarded them with an imminent victory.**}[Surat al-Fat-h: 18]

4. The pillars of Islam

Islam has five main pillars which a Muslim must fulfill in order to be a true Muslim. They are:

a. First Pillar: The testimony that there is no god worthy of worship, but Allah and that Muhammad is the Messenger of Allah

It is the first word to be pronounced by a person embracing Islam. He should say: **"I bear witness that there is no god worthy of worship, but Allah and that Muhammad is the slave and Messenger of Allah"** believing in all its meanings, which we have explained above.

He should believe that Allah is the One and Only God Who did not beget and was not begotten, and there is none like unto Him; that He is the Creator and everything else is created; and that He alone is the God worthy of being worshiped, and there is no god or lord but Him. He should also believe that Muhammad is the slave and Messenger of Allah, to whom the revelation came down from heaven, conveying Allah's commands and prohibitions; and that we should believe him in whatever he reported and obey him in what he commanded or prohibited.

b. Second Pillar: Establishing prayer

In prayer, the features of servitude and submission to Allah Almighty are manifest. A servant stands humble, reciting verses from the Qur'an and extols his Lord by different kinds of Dhikr (remembrance of Allah) and praise. He bows down and prostrates himself to the Creator, privately invoking Him and asking from His great bounty. So, prayer is a link between a servant and his Lord Who created him and knows his secret and open matters. Prayer wins one the love, nearness, and pleasure of Allah Almighty. Whoever abandons it out of arrogance incurs the wrath and curse of Allah and becomes an apostate.

The obligatory prayers are five every day, comprising standing and the recitation of Surat al-Fātihah:{**In the name of Allah, the Most Compassionate, the Most Merciful. All praise be to Allah, the Lord of the worlds, the Most Compassionate, the Most Merciful, Master of the Day of Judgment. You are alone we worship, and You are alone we ask for help. Guide us to the straight path, the path of those whom You have blessed; not of those who incurred Your Wrath, or of those who went astray.}[Surat al-Fātihah: 1-7]**In addition to reciting some other verses from the Qur'an, as well as bowing down, prostrating, supplicating, making Takbīr by saying: "Allāhu Akbar" (Allah is the Most Great), exalting Allah in bowing by saying: "Subhāna Rabbi al-'Azhīm" (Glory be to my Lord, the Majestic), and in prostration by saying: "Subhāna Rabbi al-A'la" (Glory be to my Lord, the Most High).

Before performing prayer, a Muslim should be free from impurities (urine and excrement) in his body, clothes, and the place of prayer. He should make ablution with water, washing his face and hands and wiping over his head and then washing his feet.

If he is ritually impure (due to sexual intercourse), he should take a bath, washing his whole body.

c. Third Pillar: Zakah

It is a specific percentage - 2.5% of capital assets - which Allah Almighty ordained on the rich to be given to the poor and needy and all those who are entitled to it in the community. It aims at fulfilling people's needs and ending their poverty.

This pillar is a cause of spreading social solidarity in the society and fostering love, friendliness, and cooperation among its members. It helps eliminate hatred and rancor felt by the poor and the underprivileged towards the rich and wealthy. It also plays a key role in the growth and prosperity of economy and the movement of money in a right way, thus reaching all sections of the society. Zakah is due on properties of all kinds:

money, cattle, fruits, grains, goods, etc. There are different percentages on capital assets of each kind.

d. Fourth Pillar: Fasting the month of Ramadān

Fasting is to abstain from eating, drinking, and having sexual intercourse with wives from dawn to sunset with the intention of worshiping Allah.

Ramadān, in which fasting is due, is the ninth lunar month. It is also the month in which the revelation of the Qur'an to Prophet Muhammad (may Allah's peace and blessings be upon him) started.

Allah Almighty says:{**Ramadān is a month in which the Qur'an was sent down as a guidance for mankind and as clear signs that show the right way and distinguish between right and wrong. So, whoever of you witnesses this month, should fast.**}[Surat al-Baqarah: 185]Among the great benefits of fasting is being accustomed to patience and boosting one's piety and faith in the heart. This is because fasting is a secret between a servant and his Lord. When one is alone, he can eat and drink without anyone knowing about it. So, when he refrains from that in worship and obedience to Allah Almighty alone, with no partner, knowing that only Allah watches over this act of worship, this increases his faith and sense of heedfulness. That is why the reward of the fasting people will be great. There is even a special gate in Paradise for them, called Ar-Rayyān.Outside Ramadān, a Muslim can observe voluntary fasting any day throughout the year, except for the two days of Eid al-Fitr and Eid al-Ad-ha.[Surat al-Baqarah: 185]

Among the great benefits of fasting is being accustomed to patience and boosting one's piety and faith in the heart. This is because fasting is a secret between a servant and his Lord. When one is alone, he can eat and drink without anyone knowing about it. So, when he refrains from that in worship and obedience to Allah Almighty alone, with no partner, knowing that only Allah watches over this act of worship, this increases his faith and sense of heedfulness. That is why the reward of the fasting people will be great. There is even a special gate in Paradise for them, called Ar-Rayyān.

Outside Ramadān, a Muslim can observe voluntary fasting any day throughout the year, except for the two days of Eid al-Fitr and Eid al-Ad-ha.

e. Fifth Pillar: Performing Hajj

It is obligatory upon a Muslim to perform Hajj once in a lifetime. He can do more than that voluntarily. Allah Almighty says:{**Pilgrimage to the House is a duty owed to Allah upon all people who are able to make their way to it**} [Surat Āl 'Imrān: 97]To perform Hajj, a Muslim travel to the designated places of the rituals in Makkah during the month of Hajj, namely the last Hijri lunar month. Before entering Makkah, he has to take off his usual clothes and wear the clothing of Ihrām (ritual state of consecration), two white garments.

Then, the pilgrim performs different rituals of Hajj, such as Tawāf (circumambulation) around the Ka'bah, Sa'y (walking) between Safa and Marwah, standing at 'Arafah, and spending the night at Muzdalifah.

Hajj is the biggest gathering of Muslims on earth, where the spirit of brotherliness, mercy, and sincerity prevails among them. Their clothing is the same, and so are their rituals. There is no superiority for one over another except in terms of piety. The reward of Hajj is great as stated by the Prophet (may Allah's peace and blessings be upon him):"Whoever performs Hajj without having sexual intercourse or committing sins will come out of his sins like the day he was born." [4]

"Whoever performs Hajj without having sexual intercourse or committing sins will come out of his sins like the day he was born." 4

---

[4] Narrated by Al-Bukhāri (2/164) in the Book of Hajj, Chapter: merit of the accepted Hajj

5. The Pillars of Faith

As we are now aware that the pillars of Islam are its apparent rituals that a Muslim should accept and perform to indicate his acceptance of Islam, we should also know that there are other pillars pertaining to the heart, in which a Muslim should believe in order for his Islam to be sound. They are called "the pillars of faith". The greater they are in a Muslim's heart, the higher he goes up the ranks of faith and the worthier he becomes of being one of the believing servants of Allah, a degree higher than that of being a mere Muslim. Every believer is a Muslim, but not every Muslim has reached the degree of believers.

He certainly has the basis of faith, but he may not possess perfect faith.

The pillars of faith are six:

It is to believe in Allah, His angels, His books, His messengers, the Last Day, and destiny, the pleasant and unpleasant aspects thereof.

First Pillar: belief in Allah, and as a result one's heart gets filled with love and reverence for Allah Almighty, with humility and submission towards Him, and with obedience to His commands alone, with no partner. Likewise, one's heart becomes full of fear from Allah and hope for His mercy and reward. Thus, one becomes from the pious servants of Allah who adhere to His straight path.

Second Pillar: belief in the angels; that they are servants of Allah who were created from light, that they are in the heavens and the earth, and are great in number that none can count them except for Allah, and that they are innately disposed to engage in worship, Dhikr, and glorification of Allah. They glorify Him day and night tirelessly.**{Who never disobey whatever Allah commands and do whatever they are commanded.}** [Surat at-Tahrīm: 6]Each angel has his special task for which Allah Almighty created him. Some of them are entrusted with bearing the Throne, some with taking out souls, and some with bringing down the divine revelation from heaven, which is the task of Gabriel (peace be upon him), the best among them all, in addition to the keepers of Paradise and Hell. There are other angels who love the believers and frequently supplicate Allah and ask forgiveness for them.

Third Pillar: belief in the books revealed by Allah

A Muslim believes that Allah Almighty revealed books to whomever He wills from His messengers, containing true information and just commands from Him. This includes the belief that Allah revealed the Torah to Moses, the Gospel to Jesus, the Pslams to David, and the Scrolls to Abraham; and that these books no longer exist today in the way they were originally revealed. The Muslim also believes that Allah revealed the Qur'an to the final Prophet, Muhammad (may Allah's peace and blessings be upon him); that its verses were sent down successively over a period of 23 years; and that Allah has preserved it from distortions and alterations:**{It is We Who have sent down the Reminder, and it is We Who will preserve it.}[Surat al-Hijr: 9]**

Fourth Pillar: Belief in the Messengers

We have already talked about this in detail. Prophets were sent to all nations throughout history, calling people to one religion and one God Who is the only deity worthy of worship, and warning them of disbelief, polytheism, and disobedience to Allah.**{There has never been any community except that a warner came to it.}[Surat Fātir: 24]**They were humans, just like other people, who were chosen by Allah to convey His message:**{We have sent revelation to you [O Prophet] just as We revealed to Noah and the prophets after him. We also sent revelation to Abraham, Ishmael, Isaac, Jacob and his descendants, and to Jesus, Job, Jonah, Aaron, and Solomon, and We gave David the Psalms. There are messengers whose stories We have already mentioned to you, and messengers We have not mentioned to you. And Allah spoke to Moses directly. These messengers were sent as bearers of glad tidings and as warners, so that the people may have no excuse before Allah after [the coming of] the messengers. For Allah is All-Mighty, All-Wise.}[Surat an-Nisā': 163-165]**A Muslim believes in, loves, and supports all prophets, without making any distinction between them. Whoever disbelieves in one of them or curses or reviles him has indeed disbelieved in all of them.

The best and most meritorious among them and the one with the highest rank in the sight of Allah Almighty is Muhammad, the final Prophet (may Allah's peace and blessings be upon him).

Fifth Pillar: Belief in the Last Day

and that Allah Almighty will resurrect people from their graves and gather all of them on the Day of Judgment so as to hold them accountable for their deeds in worldly life:{The Day when the earth will be changed to another earth and so will the heavens, and all will appear before Allah, the One, the Subjugator.}[Surat Ibrāhim: 48]

{When the sky breaks apart, and when the stars fall, scattered, and when the seas burst forth, and when the graves are overturned, then each soul will come to know what it has done or what it has left undone.}[Surat al-Infitār: 1-5]

{Does man not see that We have created him from a sperm drop, then he becomes a clear adversary, producing arguments against Us while forgetting his own creation. He says, "Who can give life to the bones after they have crumbled to dust? «Say, "The One Who created them in the first place will give life to them, for He has full knowledge of every created being; the One Who made for you fire out of the green tree, with which you kindle your fires. «Is not the One Who created the heavens and earth able to create the like of these [people]? Yes indeed, for He is the Creator of all, the All-Knowing. Whenever He wills something to be, He only says to it, "Be", and it is.So glory be to the One in Whose Hand is the dominion of everything, and to Him you will all be returned.}[Surat Yasīn: 77 -83]

{We will place the scales of justice on the Day of Resurrection, and no soul will be wronged in the least. Even if a deed is the weight of a mustard seed, we will bring it forth. Sufficient are We as Reckoners.}[Surat al-Anbiyā': 47]{So whoever does an atom's weight of good will see it, and whoever does an atom's weight of evil will see it.}[Surat az-Zalzalah: 7-8]

The gates of Hellfire will be opened for those who deserve Allah's wrath and painful punishment, and the gates of Paradise will be opened for the believers who act rightly and do good.{And the angels will receive them [saying], "This is your Day that you were promised".}[Surat al-Anbiyā': 103]

{Those who disbelieved will be driven to Hell in groups, until when they reach it, its gates will be opened and its keepers will say to them, "Did there not come to you messengers from among you, reciting the verses of your Lord and warning you of your meeting of this Day?" They will say, "Yes indeed, but the decree of punishment has come to pass against the disbelievers." It will be said, "Enter the gates of Hell, abiding therein forever." What a terrible abode for the arrogant! But those who feared their Lord will be led to Paradise in groups, until when they reach it, its gates will be wide open, and its keepers will say to them, "Peace be upon you. You have done well, so enter it, abiding forever. «They will say, "All praise be to Allah Who has fulfilled His promise to us and made us inherit the land to dwell wherever we please in Paradise." How excellent is the reward of those who do [good]!}[Surat az-Zumar: 71-74]Paradise has such bliss that no eye has ever seen, no ear has ever heard, and no human mind has ever imagined.{No soul knows what delights are kept hidden for them as a reward for what they used to do. Is one who is a believer like one who is an evildoer? They are not equal. As for those who believe and do righteous deeds, they will have gardens to dwell in, as an accommodation for what they used to do. But those who are rebellious, their abode will be the Fire. Every time they try to escape from it, they will be driven back into it, and it will be said to them, "Taste the punishment of the Fire which you used to deny."}[Surat as-Sajdah: 17-20]

{The likeness of Paradise promised to the righteous is that of a [garden which has] rivers of fresh water; rivers of milk the taste of which never changes; rivers of wine delicious to drink; and rivers of pure honey. They will have therein all kinds of fruit and forgiveness from their Lord. Can they be like those who will abide in the Fire forever and will be given boiling water to drink that tears apart their intestines?}[Surat Muhammad: 15]

{Indeed, the righteous will be in gardens and bliss, enjoying what their Lord has given them, and their Lord protected them from the punishment of the Blazing Fire. «Eat and drink pleasantly for what you used to do, reclining on lined up couches". And We will marry them to houris of wide beautiful eyes.}[Surat at-Tū 17-20]

May Allah make us all among the dwellers of Paradise.

Sixth Pillar: Belief in destiny; the pleasant and unpleasant aspects thereof,

and that every movement in the universe is predestined by Allah Almighty.{No calamity befalls the earth or yourselves, but it is already written in a Record before We bring it into existence. That is indeed easy for Allah.}[Surat al-Hadīd: 22]

{Indeed, we have created everything according to a determined measure.}[Surat al-Qamar: 49]{Do you not know that Allah knows all that is in the heaven and on earth? That is all [written] in a Record. This is indeed easy for Allah.}[Surat al-Hajj: 70]Whoever believes in and properly fulfills these six pillars becomes one of the believing servants of Allah. People generally have varying degrees of faith, with some higher than others. The highest degree of faith is Ihsān (excellence), which is to "worship Allah as if you could see Him; if you cannot see Him, He indeed sees you." [5]Those are the elite among people who will reach the highest ranks in Paradise, in Al-Firdaws.

6. The teachings and morality of Islam

a. The Commands

We will briefly present here some of the morals and ethics of Islam which it instills into the Muslim society. We derive them directly from the main sources of Islam, namely the Qur'an and the Prophet's Hadīths.

First: Truthfulness of speech:

Islam obliges its followers to speak the truth and considers the truthfulness of speech as an inseparable trait of Muslims that they can by no means give up. It strongly warns them against lying and seeks to alienate them from it using the most profound and clear terms. Allah Almighty says:**{O you who believe, fear Allah and be with those who are truthful.}[Surat at-Tawbah: 119]**The Messenger of Allah (may Allah's peace and blessings be upon him) said: **"Adhere to truthfulness, for truthfulness leads to righteousness and righteousness leads to Paradise. A man will keep speaking the truth and striving to speak the truth until he is recorded with Allah as the most truthful. Beware of lying, for lying leads to wickedness and wickedness leads to Hellfire. A man will keep telling lies and striving to tell lies until he is recorded with Allah as a liar."** [6]

Lying is not a trait of the believers, but of the hypocrites [7]. The Prophet (may Allah's peace and blessings be upon him) said: "The signs of the hypocrite are three: when he speaks, he lies; when he makes a promise, he breaks it; and when he is entrusted with something he betrays the trust." [8] 5

Hence, the noble Companions assumed the trait of truthfulness so much that one of them said: "We did not know telling lies during the Prophet's lifetime."

---

[5] The hypocrite is the one who displays Islam, but in his heart, he does not embrace Islam or believe in it.

Second: Fulfillment of trusts, promises, and covenants, and acting justly among people:

Allah Almighty says:{Indeed, Allah commands you to return trusts to their owners, and when you judge between people, judge with justice.} [Surat an-Nisā': 58]He also says:{And fulfill the covenant, for you will certainly be questioned about the covenant. Give full measure when you measure, and weigh with accurate scales; that is fair and best in the end.}[Surat al-Isrā': 34-35]

Praising the believers, Allah Almighty says:{those who fulfill the covenant of Allah and do not break the pledge.}[Surat ar-Ra'd: 20]

Third: Being humble and refraining from arrogance:

The Prophet (may Allah's peace and blessings be upon him) was the most humble among people. He would sit among his Companions like one of them and hate that people should stand for him when he arrived at a place. A person needing something would take him by the hand and walk together, and the Prophet (may Allah's peace and blessings be upon him) would not turn him down; rather, he would fulfill his need. The Prophet (may Allah's peace and blessings be upon him) instructed people to be modest, saying: "Indeed, Allah has revealed to me that you should humble yourselves to one another. One should neither hold himself above another nor transgress against another." [6]

Fourth: Generosity and spending in charitable causes:

Allah Almighty says:{Whatever wealth you spend in charity, it is for your own good – as long as you do so seek Allah's pleasure. And whatever wealth you spend in charity, you will be rewarded in full, and you will not be wronged.}[Surat al-Baqarah: 272]Allah praises the believers saying:{And they give food, despite their love for it, to the

---

[6] Narrated by Muslim (17/200) the Book of Paradise, Chapter: traits by which the people of Paradise are recognized

needy, the orphans, and the captives.}[Surat al-Insān: 8]Generosity was a trait of the Prophet (may Allah's peace and blessings be upon him) and of the believers who follow his example. He would always give all the money he had in charity. Jābir, one of the Prophet's Companions, said: «The Messenger of Allah (may Allah's peace and blessings be upon him) was never asked anything and said 'no'. «He urged people to honor guests, saying: **"Whoever believes in Allah and the Last Day should honor his guest; whoever believes in Allah and the Last Day should maintain his kinship ties; and whoever believes in Allah and the Last Day should speak good or keep silent."** [10]

Fifth: Patience and enduring harm:

Allah Almighty says:{**And be patient with whatever befalls you. This is a matter of firm resolve.**}[SuratLuqmān:17]He also says:{**O you who believe, seek help in patience and prayer, for Allah is with those who are patient.**}[Surat al-Baqarah: 153]And He says:{**And We will surely grant those who remain steadfast their reward according to the best of their deeds.**}[Surat an-Nahl: 96]The Prophet (may Allah's peace and blessings be upon him) was remarkably patient, enduring harm and not returning evil with evil. As he called his people to Islam, they hurt and beat him, injuring him. He wiped the blood off his face and said:**"O Allah, forgive my people for they do not know."** [11]

Sixth: Modesty:

A Muslim is a chaste and modest person. Modesty is one of the branches of faith, and it prompts one to act virtuously and prevents one from obscenity and immorality both in words and deeds. The Prophet (may Allah's peace and blessings be upon him) said: **"Modesty brings nothing but good."**[12]

"Modesty brings nothing but good." 7

---

[7] Narrated by Al-Bukhāri in the Book of courtesy, Chapter: modesty (8/35)

Seventh: Dutifulness to one's parents:

Dutifulness, kindness, and humility towards one's parents represent one of the fundamental duties in Islam. This duty becomes even more due as parents grow older and more in need for their children. Commanding dutifulness to parents and affirming their rights, Allah Almighty says:{**Your Lord has ordained that you worship none but Him and show kindness to parents. If one or both of them reach old age in your care, do not say to them a word of annoyance nor scold them, rather speak to them noble words, and lower to them the wing of humility out of mercy, and say, "My Lord, have mercy upon them as they raised me when I was small."**}[Surat alsrā': 23-24]

He also says:{**We have enjoined upon man kindness to his parents. His mother bore him in weakness upon weakness, and his weaning took place within two years. Be grateful to Me and to your parents. To Me is the final return.**}[Surat Luqmān: 14]

A man once asked the Prophet (may Allah's peace and blessings be upon him): "Who is more worthy of my good companionship?" He said: «Your mother." The man asked: "Then who?" He said: "Your mother." He asked: "Then who?" He said: "Your mother." He asked: "Then who?" He said: "Your father." [13] 8

Hence, Islam enjoins the Muslim to obey his parents in whatever they ask him to do, unless a sin is involved, for none should be obeyed when it comes to disobeying Allah. Allah Almighty says:{**But if they strive to make you associate partners with Me of what you have no knowledge, then do not obey them. Yet keep company with them in this world with kindness.**}[Surat Luqmān:15]Islam also instructs one to show respect and humility towards them, to honor them with words and deeds, to be kind to them in all ways, like providing them with food, clothes, and medicine, if needed, and to keep any harm away from them. One is also required to supplicate Allah and ask His forgiveness for them, fulfill their promises, and honor their friends.

---

[8] Narrated by Al-Bukhāri in the Book of courtesy, Chapter: who among people is the most entitled to good companionship (8/2)

Eighth: Treating people with good morals:

The Prophet (may Allah's peace and blessings be upon him) said: «The most perfect believers in faith are those with most excellent morals." [14] 9

In another Hadīth, the Prophet (may Allah's peace and blessings be upon him) said: "Among the dearest and closest of you to me on the Day of Judgment are those with the most excellent morals." [15] 10

Allah Almighty in describing His Prophet (may Allah's peace and blessings be upon him), says:{Indeed, you are of a great moral character.} [Surat al-Qalam: 4]In another Hadīth, the Prophet (may Allah's peace and blessings be upon him) said: «Indeed, I have been sent to complete the noble morals." [16]So, a Muslim should be noble-mannered and kind towards his parents, as we have mentioned, and towards his children, raising them in a good way, teaching them the morality and rulings of Islam, keeping them away from whatever could harm them in this life and in the Hereafter, and spending on them till they grow up and can rely upon themselves and earn their living. Likewise, he should deal with noble morals with his wife, brothers, sisters, relatives, neighbors, and all people. He should wish for his fellow Muslims what he wishes for himself and uphold good ties with his relatives and neighbors, revering the elderly, showing compassion towards the young, and visiting and supporting the distressed among them - in compliance with the verse that says:{Be kind to parents, relatives, orphans, the needy, near and distant

---

[9] Narrated by Abu Dāwūd in the Book of Sunnah, Chapter: the evidence on its increase and decrease (5/6); and At-Tirmidhi in the Book of nursing, Chapter: what is reported concerning the woman's right over her husband (3/457); At-Tirmidhi classified it as Hasan Sahīh (sound authentic) and regarding Al-Albāni's judgment: see "Sahīh Abi Dāwūd" (3/886)

[10] Narrated by Al-Bukhāri in the Book of virtues, Chapter: character of the Prophet (may Allah's peace and blessings be upon him) (4/230) with the wording (Indeed, the best among you are those with the most excellent morals)

neighbors, close friends, wayfarers.}[Surat an-Nisā': 36]The Prophet (may Allah's peace and blessings be upon him) said: "Whoever believes in Allah and the Last Day should not hurt his neighbor." [17]11

Ninth: Jihad in the cause of Allah to support the oppressed, establish the truth, and spread justice:

Allah Almighty says:{Fight in the way of Allah against those who fight you, but do not transgress, for Allah does not like transgressors.}[Surat al-Baqarah: 190]He also says:{Why is it that you do not fight in the way of Allah and for the sake of the oppressed men, women, and children who say, "Our Lord, take us out of this town of oppressive people, and grant us from Yourself a protector and grant us from Yourself a helper."?}[Surat an-Nisā': 75]So, the Islamic Jihad aims at establishing the truth, spreading justice among people, and fighting those who oppress people, persecute them, and prevent them from worshiping Allah and embracing Islam. On the other hand, it rejects the idea of coercing people to enter Islam. Allah Almighty says:{There is no compulsion in religion.}[Surat al-Baqarah: 256]

During battles, a Muslim is not allowed to kill a woman, a child, or an old person, rather he should only fight the wrongful combatants.

Whoever gets killed in the cause of Allah is a martyr and for him is a great reward and status with Allah Almighty, who says:{Never think of those who are killed in Allah's way as dead. Rather, they are alive with their Lord, receiving provision, rejoicing in what Allah has given them of His bounty, and delighted for those who have yet to join them, of those whom they left behind, that they will have no fear, nor will they grieve.}[Surat Āl 'Imrān: 169-170]

Tenth: Supplication, Dhikr, and Qur'an recitation:

---

[11] Narrated by Imam Ahmad in "Al-Musnad" (17/80) and Ahmad Shākir said its Isnād is authentic; Al-Bukhāri in "Al-Adab"; Al-Bayhaqi in "Shu'ab al-Imān"; and Al-Hākim in "Al-Mustadrak"

The greater a person's faith is, the closer he is to his Lord and the more he supplicates and implores Him to fulfill his needs in life and forgive his sins and elevate his rank in the Hereafter. Indeed, Allah is Generous, and He loves His servants to ask of Him as He says:**{When My slaves ask you concerning Me, I am indeed near. I respond to the call of the supplicant when he calls upon Me.}[Surat al-Baqarah: 186]**Allah answers supplications, if they are good for the supplicants, and rewards them for supplicating Him. Another trait of the believers is that they remember Allah Almighty frequently, day and night, both secretly and in public. They glorify Him with all kinds of glorification and Dhikr, like saying: "Subhānallāh" (glory be to Allah), "al-Hamdulillāh" (praise be to Allah), "Lā ilāha illallāh" (there is no god but Allah), and "Allāhu Akbar" (Allah is the Greatest). Allah Almighty gives abundant rewards for that as the Prophet (may Allah's peace and blessings be upon him) said: «The Mufarridūn have gone ahead." They said: "Who are the Mufarridūn O Messenger of Allah?" He said: "They are those men and women who remember Allah frequently." [18]Allah Almighty says:**{O you who believe, remember Allah much, and glorify Him morning and evening.} [Surat al-Ahzāb: 41-42]**. In another verse, Allah Almighty says: **{Therefore remember Me; I will remember you. Be grateful to Me, and do not be ungrateful.}[Surat al-Baqarah: 152]**Dhikr includes recitation of the Book of Allah, the Noble Qur'an. The more one recites it and ponders on its meanings, the higher his rank will be in the sight of his Lord.

On the Day of Judgment, the following will be said to the Qur'an reciter: «Read and ascend (in ranks) and recite as you used to recite when you were in the world, for your rank will be at the last verse you recite." [19] "Read and ascend (in ranks) and recite as you used to recite when you were in the world, for your rank will be at the last verse you recite." 12

---

[12] Narrated by Abu Dāwūd (1464) and this is his wording, At-Tirmidhi (2914), An-Nasā'i in "As-Sunan al-Kubra" (8056), and Ahmad (6799)

Eleventh: Seeking religious knowledge, teaching it to others, and calling them to it:

The Prophet (may Allah's peace and blessings be upon him) said: «Whoever follows a path seeking knowledge, Allah facilitates for him a path to Paradise. Indeed, the angels put down their wings for the seeker of knowledge out of pleasure with what he does." [20] 13

In another Hadīth, the Prophet (may Allah's peace and blessings be upon him) said: «The best of you are those who learn the Qur'an and teach it to others." [21]In another Hadīth, the Prophet (may Allah's peace and blessings be upon him) said: «Indeed, the angels invoke Allah's blessings upon the one who teaches good to people." [22]In another Hadīth, the Prophet (may Allah's peace and blessings be upon him) said: «Whoever calls to guidance will have a reward similar to that of those who act upon it, without diminishing their reward in any way." [23] 14

Allah Almighty says:{Who is better in speech than one who calls to Allah, does righteous deeds, and says, "I am one of the Muslims [submitting to Allah]"?}[Surat Fussilat: 33]

Twelfth: Contentment with the judgment of Allah and His Messenger:

Not showing discontent with anything prescribed by Allah Almighty, for He is the Best Judge and the Most Merciful Lord from Whom nothing in the earth or heaven is hidden, and Whose judgment is not affected by the whims of His servants or the greed of tyrants. Out of His mercy, He has

---

[13] Narrated by At-Tirmidhi in the Book of knowledge, Chapter: the merit of Fiqh in worship (4/153); Abu Dāwūd in the Book of knowledge, Chapter: urging people to seek knowledge (4/5857); and Ibn Mājah in "Al-Muqaddimah" (1/81); and it was classified as Sahīh (authentic) by Al-Albāni in "Sahīh al-Jāmi'" (5/302)

[14] Narrated by Al-Bukhāri in the Book of virtues, Chapter: the best of you are those who learn the Qur'an and teach it to others (6/236)

prescribed for His servants what serves their interests in this life and in the Hereafter and He has not charged them with anything beyond their capacity. Our servitude to Him entails that we refer for judgment to His Shariah concerning all matters, with complete heart-felt contentment.

Allah Almighty says:{But no, by your Lord, they will not believe until they accept you [O Prophet] as judge in their disputes and find no discomfort within their hearts about your judgments but accept them wholeheartedly.}[Surat an-Nisā': 65]He also says:{Do they seek the judgment of the times of ignorance? Who could be better than Allah in judgment for people who are certain in faith?}[Surat al-Mā'idah: 50]

b. The Unlawful and Prohibited Things

First: Polytheism: Devoting any form of servitude to other than Allah Almighty:

Examples include prostrating to other than Allah, invoking other than Allah and asking him for the fulfillment of needs, offering sacrifices to other than Allah, or devoting any form of servitude to other than Allah. The invoked one may be alive or dead, and it may be a grave, an idol, a stone, a tree, a king, a prophet, a pious person, an animal, or the like. All of this falls under polytheism which Allah does not forgive unless the perpetrator repents and reverts to Islam.

Allah Almighty says: {Allah does not forgive associating partners with Him but forgives anything less than that for whom He wills. Whoever associates partners with Allah has indeed committed a grave sin.} [Surat an-Nisā': 48] A Muslim worship none but Allah, invokes none but Allah, and humbly submits to none but Him. Allah Almighty says: {Say, "Indeed, my prayer, my sacrifice, my living and my dying are all for Allah, Lord of the worlds. He has no partner. This is what I have been commanded, and I am the first to submit to Allah."} [Surat al-An'ām: 162-163]

One of the forms of polytheism is to believe that Allah has a wife or a son - far exalted be He above that - or to believe that there are other gods disposing of the affairs of this universe. {If there had been gods besides Allah in the heavens and earth, both realms would have fallen in disorder. Glory be to Allah – Lord of the Throne – far above what they ascribe [to Him].} [Surat al-Anbiyā': 22]

Second: Magic, divination, and claiming to know the unseen:

Magic and divination are disbelief. Indeed, a magician cannot be a magician except through his connection with the devils and worshiping them apart from Allah. Hence, it is not permissible for a Muslim to go to magicians or soothsayers or believe their claims about knowing the unseen or any event they allege will happen in the future.

Allah Almighty says: {Say, "No one in the heavens and earth has knowledge of the unseen except Allah."}[Surat an-Naml: 65]

He also says:{[He is] Knower of the unseen, He does not reveal His unseen to anyone, except the messenger whom He chooses, then He appoints angel-guards before him and behind him.}[Surat al-Jinn: 26-27]

Third: Injustice:

Injustice is a broad term that comprises many evil acts and bad traits that impact people. Falling under this is injustice to oneself, injustice to others, injustice to society, and injustice even to enemies. Allah Almighty says:{And do not let the hatred of a people lead you away from justice. Be just; that is closer to righteousness.}[Surat al-Mā'idah: 8]Allah Almighty informs us that He does not love the unjust. In a Qudsi (divine) Hadīth, Allah Almighty said:"O My servants, I have forbidden injustice for Myself and made it forbidden amongst you; so, do not wrong one another." [24]In another Hadīth, the Prophet (may Allah's peace and blessings be upon him) said: "Support your brother whether he is oppressor or oppressed." A man said: "O Messenger of Allah, I should support him if he is oppressed, but how should I support him if he is oppressor?" The Prophet (may Allah's peace and blessings be upon him) said: "Support him by preventing him from oppression." [25] 15

Fourth: Killing the soul made inviolable by Allah without right:

This is a serious crime in the religion of Islam for which Allah Almighty threatens with painful punishment and has prescribed the toughest penalties in this world, namely killing the killer unless the murdered person's heirs pardon the murderer. Allah Almighty says:{**For this reason We ordained for the Children of Israel that whoever kills a person – unless in retribution for murder or corruption in the land – it is as if he killed all mankind.**}[Surat al-Mā'idah: 32]He also says:{**But anyone who kills a believer deliberately, his punishment will be Hell, abiding therein forever; Allah will be displeased with him, and will curse him, and will prepare for him a great punishment.**}[Surat an-Nisā': 93]

Fifth: Encroaching upon people's properties:

be it by theft, usurpation, bribery, fraud, or the like. Allah Almighty says:{**As for the thief, male or female, amputate their hands as a deterrent punishment from Allah for what they have done. Allah is All-Mighty, All-Wise.**}[Surat al-Mā'idah: 38]He also says:{**Do not consume one another's property unjustly.**}[Surat al-Baqarah: 188]He also says:{**Indeed, those who consume the orphans' property unjustly, they only consume fire into their bellies, and they will burn in a Blazing Fire.**}[Surat an-Nisā': 10]

Islam strongly opposes encroachment upon people's properties and gives stern warnings about this. It prescribes harsh penalties against the perpetrators of this and similar crimes that disturb the order and security of society.

---

[15] Narrated by Muslim in the Book of righteousness, maintaining ties, and ethics, Chapter: prohibition of oppression (16/132)

Sixth: Cheating, treachery, and betrayal:

in all dealings, such as buying, selling, covenants, and the like. These are reprehensible traits that Islam forbids and warns people against.

Allah Almighty says:{**Woe to the defrauders, those who take full measure when they take from others, but they give less when they measure or weigh for them. Do they really not think that they will be resurrected for a momentous Day, a Day when people will stand before the Lord of the worlds?**}[Surat al-Mutaffifīn: 1-5]The Prophet (may Allah's peace and blessings be upon him) said: «Whoever cheats us is not one of us." [26]Allah Almighty says:{**Allah does not like the treacherous and sinful.**}[Surat an-Nisā': 107]

Seventh: Attacking people's honor

by cursing, reviling, backbiting, slandering, envying, distrusting, spying, mocking, and the like. Islam is keen to establish a clean and pure society that abounds in love, brotherliness, harmony, and cooperation. To this end, it firmly combats all social ills that lead to the disintegration of society and the appearance of rancor, hatred, and selfishness among its members.

Allah Almighty says:{**O you who believe, let not some men ridicule others, for it may be that they are better than them; nor let some women ridicule others, for it may be that they are better than them. Do not speak ill of one another, nor call one another by [offensive] nicknames. How evil is the name of wickedness after having faith! And whoever does not repent, it is they who are the wrongdoers you who believe, avoid much of the suspicion, for some suspicions are sin. Do not spy on one another, nor backbite one another. Would any of you like to eat the flesh of his dead brother? You would surely abhor it. So, fear Allah. Indeed, Allah is Accepting of Repentance, Most Merciful.**}[Surat al-Hujurāt: 11-12]Islam also strongly combats racial and class-based discrimination between members of society. In its eyes, all are equal. There is no superiority for an Arab over a non-Arab or for a white over a black except in terms of religiousness and piety. Everyone equally vies in doing good deeds. Allah Almighty says:{O mankind, we have created you from a male and a female and made you into nations and tribes so that you may recognize one another. Indeed, the most noble of you before Allah is the most righteous among you. Indeed, Allah is All-Knowing, All-Aware.}[Surat al-Hujurāt: 13]

Eighth: Gambling, drinking alcohol, and drug abuse:

Allah Almighty says:{O you who believe, intoxicants, gambling, idols and divining arrows are evil, of Satan's work; therefore, avoid such [evil], so that you may be successful. Satan only wants to create enmity and hatred between you through intoxicants and gambling, and to prevent you from remembering Allah and from prayer. Will you not then abstain?}[Surat al-Mā'idah: 90-91]

Ninth: Consuming the flesh of dead animals, blood, and pork:

and all filthy and harmful things to people. This also applies to sacrifices offered to other than Allah Almighty Who says:{O you who believe, eat of the good things We have provided for you, and be grateful to Allah, if you truly worship Him alone. He has only forbidden to you carrion, blood, the flesh of swine, and what has been sacrificed to other than Allah. But if someone is compelled by necessity – neither driven by desire nor exceeding immediate need – then there is no sin upon him; for Allah is All-Forgiving, Most Merciful.}[Surat al-Baqarah: 172-173]

Tenth: Adultery and sodomy:

Adultery is a malicious deed that ruins morals and societies and leads to mingling of lineages, loss of families, and absence of proper upbringing. Illegitimate children feel the bitterness of this crime and the hatred of society. Allah Almighty says:{**Do not go near adultery, for it is indeed a shameful act and an evil way.**}[Surat al-Isrā': 32]Adultery causes spread of sexual diseases that destroy the fabric of society. The Prophet (may Allah's peace and blessings be upon him) said:" Immorality does not prevail among any people to the extent that they commit it openly except that plague and diseases that did not exist among their predecessors will spread among them." [27] 16

Islam, therefore, instructs us to block all means leading to adultery. For example, it commands Muslims to lower their gaze, for an unlawful look constitutes the first step towards adultery, and Islam also commands women to wear Hijab and modest clothing and stick to chastity, thus preserving society from this vice. On the other hand, Islam urges and encourages people to get married and promises reward even for this sexual pleasure that the husband and wife engage in, as this helps establish chaste and dignified families that are well qualified for the successful upbringing of today's child and tomorrow's man.

Eleventh: Consuming usury:

Usury damages the economy, and it involves exploitation of people's need for money, whether for doing business or fulfilling basic living needs. In usury, money is lent to someone for a fixed period of time in return for an increase to be paid along with the repayment of the debt. A usurer exploits the poor person's need for money and burdens him with accumulative debts added to the original amount.

A usurer takes advantage of the needs of traders, manufacturers, farmers, and others who affect the economy.

He exploits their need for cash and imposes upon them an extra amount of the profits, whereas he only lends them without sharing the risk of stagnation or loss.

If such a trader incurs a loss, debts accumulate on him, and the usurer crushes him. If they were partners, however, sharing profit and loss, one

---

[16] Narrated by Ibn Mājah in the Book of trials, Chapter: penalties (2/1333), and Al-Albāni judged it as Hasan (sound) (Sahīh Ibn Mājah) (2/370)

with his effort and the other with his money, as instructed by Islam, the wheel of the economy would keep moving for the benefit of society.

Allah Almighty says:{O you who believe, fear Allah and give up usury that is still due, if you are truly believers. But if you do not do it, then beware of a declaration of war from Allah and His Messenger. However, if you repent, you may retain your capital – neither harming nor suffering harm. If the debtor is in hardship, give him respite until it is easy for him to pay back. But if you waive it as charity, that is better for you, if only you knew.}[Surat al-Baqarah: 278-280]

Twelfth: Avarice and stinginess:

It denotes selfishness and self-love. A miser hoards wealth and refuses to pay his Zakah to the poor and the needy, denying his society and rejecting the principle of cooperation and brotherliness which Allah and His Messenger commanded. Allah Almighty says:{Those who greedily withhold what Allah has given them of His grace, should not think that it is good for them, rather it is bad for them; their necks will be chained by what they greedily withheld on the Day of Resurrection. To Allah belongs the inheritance of the heavens and earth, and Allah is All-Aware of what you do.}[Surat Āl 'Imrān: 180]

Thirteenth: Lying and false testimony:

We have previously cited the Prophet's Hadīth: "Indeed, lying leads to immorality, and immorality leads to Hellfire, and a man would continue to lie and be keen on lying until he is recorded in the sight of Allah as a liar. One of the types of reprehensible lying is false testimony. The Prophet (may Allah's peace and blessings be upon him) went to great lengths to keep people away from it and warn them of its evil consequences. He said to his Companions loudly: «Shall I inform you of the gravest major sins? Associating partners with Allah and undutifulness to one's parents." Then, he sat up after being in a state of reclining and added: "And beware of the false testimony; and beware of the false testimony." [28]He kept repeating his statement so as to warn the Ummah against committing this sin.

Fourteenth: Arrogance, self-conceit, self-admiration, and vanity:

Arrogance, self-conceit, and vanity are ugly and reprehensible traits frowned upon in the religion of Islam. Allah Almighty informs us that He does not love the arrogant. He says about them:{Is there not in Hell an abode for the arrogant?}[Surat az-Zumar: 60] A self-conceited, self-admiring, and an arrogant person is hated by Allah Almighty and hated by people.

c. Repentance of prohibited things

A Muslim should be so careful to avoid these major sins and aforementioned prohibitions, for he will be recompensed in the Hereafter for any act he does, with reward for goodness and punishment for evil.

But if a Muslim falls into any of these prohibitions, he should hasten to repent of it and turn to his Lord and ask for His forgiveness. If his repentance is sincere, he should give up the sin, feel regretful for doing it, resolve not to repeat it, and if the sin involves injustice to someone, he should return the right to its owner or ask him for pardon. This way, his repentance will be a true one and Allah will accept it and forgive his sin. Indeed, a person who truly repents of a sin is like one who has not sinned in the first place.

And he should often ask Allah for forgiveness. Indeed, all Muslims should frequently ask for Allah's forgiveness for their misdeeds, small or great. Allah Almighty says:{I said, 'Seek forgiveness from your Lord. Indeed, He is Most Forgiving.}[Surat Nūh10] Frequently asking Allah for forgiveness and returning to Him in repentance is a trait of the humble believers. Allah Almighty says:{Say [Allah says], "O My slaves who have transgressed against themselves, do not despair of Allah's mercy, for indeed Allah forgives all sins. He is indeed the All-Forgiving, the Most Merciful. Turn to your Lord [in repentance] and submit to Him before the punishment comes upon you, for then you will not be helped."}[Surat az-Zumar: 53-54]

d. The Muslims' care about the authentic transmission of this religion:

Since it is the Prophet's statements, actions, and approvals that clarify Allah's words and explain the commands and prohibitions in Islam, the Muslims paid great attention to the authenticity of the transmission of the Hadīths reported from the Prophet (may Allah's peace and blessings be upon him), and they exerted tremendous efforts in ridding these Hadīths of additions that were not said by the Prophet and in revealing the statements falsely attributed to him. To this end, they laid down the most accurate rules and systems to be observed in the transmission of these Hadīths from one generation to another.

We will briefly talk about this field of knowledge - the science of Hadīth - to make the reader aware of what made the Muslim Ummah distinct from other religions, as Allah enabled this Ummah to preserve their religion pure and untainted by lies and superstitions over the ages.

Transmitting the speech of Allah and the statements of the Prophet (may Allah's peace and blessings be upon him) relied upon two main ways:

memorization and writing down. The early Muslims were among the best people in accurate memorization and broad comprehension, because of their clear minds and sharp memories. This is a clear fact to anyone who reads their biographies. A Companion would hear a Hadīth right from the Prophet's mouth and memorize it well and then convey it to someone from the following generation (Tābi'i), who in turn would memorize and convey it to those after him. In this way, the chain of transmitting Hadīths would continue until it reached a scholar of Hadīth, who would write them down, memorize them, and collect them in a book. Then, he would read out the book to his students, who would in turn memorize and record these Hadīths and then read them out to their students and so on. The cycle kept going until these books reached all the subsequent generations in this way and manner.

Hence, any Hadīth from the Prophet (may Allah's peace and blessings be upon him) is never accepted without knowing its chain of narrators who reported it to us.

Based on this, there emerged another science that distinguished the Muslim Ummah from all other nations; namely 'Ilm ar-Rijāl (knowledge of men), or 'Ilm al-Jarh wa at-Ta'dīl (science of criticism and commendation).

This science is meant for knowing the conditions of those narrators who reported the Prophet's Hadīths to us. So, it examines their biographies, their birth and death dates, their Shaykhs and their students, and it documents their contemporary scholars, how perfect and accurate their memorization was, their truthfulness of speech, and other things of interest to the scholar of Hadīth for the purpose of verifying the authenticity of a given Hadīth reported through a certain chain of narrators.

This science is uniquely adopted by this Ummah out of the Muslims' keenness on the authenticity of any statement attributed to the Prophet (may Allah's peace and blessings be upon him). Never in history, from its very beginning to this day, have people seen such huge efforts and care about the statement of any person as they have seen with regard to the Prophet's Hadīths.

It is a broad science written down in books totally concerned with the narration of Hadīths and containing detailed biographies for thousands of narrators for the sole reason that they were the intermediaries in the transmission of the Prophet's Hadīths to the succeeding generations. This science was not established in favor of anyone, but as a balance in terms of the accuracy of criticism. It labels the liar a liar and the truthful a truthful, and likewise it classifies those with poor or strong memorization as such. To this end, they followed the most precise rules ever known to the specialists in this field.

They would not consider any Hadīth authentic unless its chain of transmission was connected, and its narrators were marked by integrity, truthfulness, and good memorization and accuracy.

The other thing in the science of Hadīth

is the multiplicity of the chains of transmission for the same Hadīth. This means that a Hadīth is reported from the Prophet (may Allah's peace and blessings be upon him) through more than one chain of narrators. So, one Hadīth may have two, three, or four Isnāds (chains of transmission) and sometimes ten or even more.

The more the chains of transmission are, the stronger the Hadīth is and the more authentically attributed to the Prophet (may Allah's peace and blessings be upon him) it is. A Hadīth narrated by more than ten reliable narrators at all levels of transmission is called "Mutawātir" (collectively transmitted) and this constitutes the best type of transmission among Muslims. The greater the significance of an issue in Islam is, like the pillars of this religion, the more the Mutawātim arrations and Isnāds about it are, and vice versa; when a certain matter falls under secondary or recommended issues, there is less attention paid to it and fewer Isnāds for the Hadīths dealing with it.

The greatest attention paid by Muslims in terms of narration and the accuracy of transmission was devoted to the Noble Qur'an. This noble book received utmost attention represented by writing it down and memorizing it, as well as perfecting its words, articulation, and recitation. It was transmitted via Isnāds through thousands and thousands over the successive generations. Hence, it has not been subject to any distortion or alteration over the years. The Mus-haf (hard copy of the Qur'an) recited in Morocco is the same as the one recited in the East or in any region around the globe, in confirmation of the verse that says: {It is We Who have sent down the Reminder, and it is We Who will preserve it.}[Surat al-Hijr: 9]

{It is We Who have sent down the Reminder, and it is We Who will preserve it.} [Surat al-Hijr: 9]

e. A last word:

This is the religion of Islam which declares Allah Almighty as the One and Only God and whose motto is "there is no god worthy of worship but Allah". This is Islam which Allah has approved as a religion for His servants.

{Today I have perfected your religion for you, completed My favor upon you, and have chosen Islam as your religion.}[Surat al-Mā'idah: 3] This is the religion of Islam other than which Allah Almighty accepts no religion from anyone.{Anyone who seeks a religion other than Islam, never will it be accepted from him; and in the Hereafter he will be among the losers.}[Surat Āl 'Imrān: 85]This is the religion of Islam which if one believes in and acts rightly, one will be among the blissful winners in Paradise.{As for those who believe and do righteous deeds, they will have gardens of Paradise as a dwelling place, abiding therein forever, never desiring to leave.}[Surat al-Kahf: 107-108] This is the religion of Islam, which does not exclusively belong to a certain group of people or a specific ethnicity. Rather, whoever believes in this religion and calls people to it becomes one of its worthy followers and the most honorable in the sight of Allah Almighty:{Indeed, the most noble of you before Allah is the most righteous among you.}[Surat al-Hujurāt: 13]

We should bring to the reader's notice certain matters that act as a barrier between people and this religion and prevent them from embracing it:

First: Ignorance about the religion of Islam in terms of its creed, Shariah, and ethics. People tend to be hostile towards what they do not know. So, the one interested in knowing Islam should read and read and read until he gets acquainted with this religion from its original sources. He should read with an unbiased and fair mind that seeks only for the truth.

Second: Fanaticism for the religion, habits, and culture in which one has grown up without thinking deeply and deliberately about whether or not this religion is true. Driven by nationalistic fanaticism, one tends to reject any other religion than the religion of one's forefathers. Indeed, fanaticism blinds eyes, deafens ears, and stiffens minds, preventing one from thinking freely and without bias, and thus one cannot distinguish the light from darkness.

Third: Personal whims and desires, which drive people's thinking and will towards what they want and ruin them without them knowing it. They prevent people from accepting the truth and submitting to it.

Fourth: The existence of some mistakes and aberrations among some Muslims, which are falsely ascribed to Islam itself, whereas this religion is totally innocent of them. It should be known to everyone that the religion of Allah is not responsible for people's errors.

The easiest way for knowing the truth and reaching guidance is to turn towards Allah Almighty with our hearts, humbly imploring Him to guide us to the straight path and the true religion which He loves and approves, and through which one attains a good life in this world and eternal bliss in the Hereafter, never followed by misery or hardship. And we should know that Allah Almighty responds to the call of a supplicant when he invokes Him as He says: {**When My slaves ask you concerning Me, I am indeed near. I respond to the call of the supplicant when he calls upon Me; so, they should respond to Me and believe in Me, so that they may be guided.**} [Surat al-Baqarah: 186].